CROCHETED SOCKS!

16 FUN-TO-STITCH PATTERNS

Janet Rehfeldt and Mary Jane Wood

Martingale®
& COMPANY

Crocheted Socks! 16 Fun-to-Stitch Patterns
© 2003 by Janet Rehfeldt and Mary Jane Wood

Martingale & Company
20205 144th Avenue NE
Woodinville, WA 98072-8478 USA
www.martingale-pub.com

Printed in China
08 07 06 05 04   8 7 6 5 4 3

Credits

President — Nancy J. Martin
CEO — Daniel J. Martin
Publisher — Jane Hamada
Editorial Director — Mary V. Green
Managing Editor — Tina Cook
Technical Editor — Ursula Reikes
Copy Editor — Ellen Balstad
Design Director — Stan Green
Illustrator — Laurel Strand
Cover & Text Designer — Shelly Garrison
Photographer — Brent Kane

Library of Congress Cataloging-in Publication Data

Rehfeldt, Janet.
    Crocheted socks! : 16 fun-to-stitch patterns / Janet Rehfeldt and Mary Jane Wood.
        p. cm.
    ISBN 1-56477-494-5
1. Crocheting—Patterns. 2. Socks. I. Wood, Mary Jane.
II. Title.
    TT825.R42 2003
    746.43'40432—dc21
                                                    2003005460

Dedication

Janet would like to dedicate this book to her family for all their support and to the memory of her grandmother Elsie Downs, who never went anywhere without a ball of yarn and needle or hook.

Mary Jane would like to dedicate this book to all the crocheters who have generously shared their knowledge and creativity with others.

Mission Statement
Dedicated to providing quality products and service
to inspire creativity.

CONTENTS

INTRODUCTION

Socks are hot, hot, hot! And crocheting your own socks is in! Yarn companies are clamoring to meet the growing demand by producing an ever-increasing range of colors, styles, and types of yarns just for socks. A visit to your local yarn shop is like a visit to wonderland. Yarn choices range from solid colors, self-striping, and confetti or dot with splashes of color, to allover colorways, Fair Isle or Jacquard patterning, and stretchy elastic. By combining different yarns and stitch patterns, you can crochet socks that are conservative, fun and frivolous, or a work of art. And now you can even buy clear plastic boots and clogs just to display your fashionably clad feet and show off your favorite pair of socks.

When Mary Jane and I began working together to design crocheted socks, we wanted to bring the shaping used for knit socks and the beautiful stitch patterns of crochet together to create comfortable, stylish, and great-fitting socks for crocheters. What started out as a pet project soon became an addiction. Now when we see a ball of yarn, the first thing we think about is whether it will make a good pair of socks.

The patterns in this book were designed for the crocheter who has some knowledge of and experience with basic crochet stitches. In order to pack many patterns into a limited amount of space, we have not provided illustrations or instructions for the basic crochet stitches. If you are unfamiliar with these stitches or a stitch in this book that is not followed by illustrated instructions, we suggest that you refer to your favorite crochet reference guide to help you make your socks.

Creating the socks for this book was a lot of fun. We hope you get as much enjoyment from crocheting our socks as we had in designing them.

SOCK BASICS

Yarn Choices

There are lots of yarns on the market today that will make wonderful socks. However, if you want your socks to wear and fit well, select sock yarns that contain some nylon (sometimes listed as polyamide); they will wear better than yarns without nylon. If you fall in love with a yarn that doesn't have nylon, you can still use it for socks. Just be sure to run a thin elastic thread or Wooly Nylon serger thread along with the sock yarn when crocheting the cuff. This will help your socks stay up better.

Reinforcing heels and toes on your socks is optional. Crocheting a reinforcement yarn into the heel or toe will give a little extra strength when socks are worn in boots and/or get a lot of wear. A few yarn companies include matching reinforcement yarn with each skein. Wooly Nylon will also work as a reinforcement thread.

Yarn amounts given in the materials section of the patterns are based on the circumference of the sock leg, the height of the sock leg, and the length of the sock foot. The length of the sock foot is based on the women's and men's shoe sizes listed in the standardized chart on page 8 and is a guideline only for the finished length of the sock foot. For women's shoe sizes over 8½ and wider than a medium width, and men's shoe sizes over 11½ and wider than a medium width, we recommend that you purchase additional yarn. A longer foot or leg length will take additional yarn. Purchase enough yarn to complete your socks.

Terrific Tools

It doesn't take any special tools or gadgets to crochet socks. The right yarn, the right-size hook, a few stitch markers, a pair of scissors, and you're on your way. However, there are some great tools and gadgets that can be helpful and fun to use.

• Crochet hooks can vary in size from one manufacturer to the next. For example, a G hook may be 4.00 mm from one manufacturer, and 4.25 mm from a different manufacturer. The hook sizes listed in the materials section of each pattern are given in both US and metric sizes, as in size E (3.5 mm). Be sure to use a hook to match the metric size, or a size to match the required gauge. If your hook does not show a millimeter size, use a needle/hook gauge, which is available at your local yarn shop, to determine the hook size.

- Stitch markers are useful in marking where to work increases, decreases, and the beginning of rounds (see "Working with Markers" on page 10).

- Row counters are handy for tracking the rows on stitch-pattern repeats and tracking the number of times you may need to increase or decrease in a pattern.

- If you tend to misplace your scissors, a thread-cutter pendant is just the ticket. It's also perfect for travel.

- The nifty new sock minder or Sockenfix by Addi holds your socks together so that you don't fall victim to the sock bandit, who seems to take only a single sock and leaves the mate lonely and adrift.

- A good tape measure is a must for taking accurate measurements and checking your gauge.

- Large, blunt-end needles are necessary for weaving in ends and finishing toes and cuffs.

Sock Construction

Sock construction is pretty basic and straightforward. The patterns in this book are crocheted from either the cuff down to the toe, referred to as *top-down socks*, or from the toe up to the cuff, referred to as *toe-up socks*. The parts of a sock consist of the cuff, leg, heel, foot, and toe.

Sock Terminology

Sock with Heel Flap and Gusset

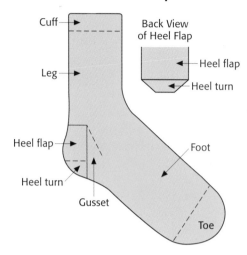

Sock with Short-Rowed Heel

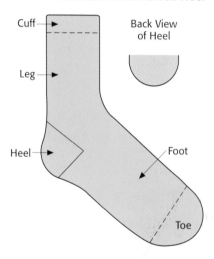

Cuffs

There are two cuff styles: cuffs with front and back post stitches worked in the round, and cuffs worked sideways with slip stitches or single crochet.

In patterns where the sock cuff is made with front and back post stitches for ribbing, we prefer to begin with a foundation double crochet rather than a standard chain. Because the sock must be able to fit over the foot, around the arch and heel, the cuff needs to be able to stretch a bit. Using a standard crochet chain will not give you the elasticity or stretch of a double crochet foundation (see page 10).

The sideways cuff is worked in rows rather than rounds, usually with single crochet or slip stitches in the back loop of the stitch. Because slip stitches tend to lie on top of the previous row or round, tilt the work slightly toward you to make the stitches a little easier to see. Work slip stitches loosely and uniform in size to keep your cuff from being uneven. Once the cuff is complete, you will crochet along the long edge of the cuff to begin the leg portion. Space your stitches evenly along the edge of the cuff for a smooth transition from the cuff to the leg.

Legs

There are two different ways in which legs are crocheted. The most common method is in the round from the top down or bottom up. The legs in Wiggly Toes on page 59 are crocheted side to side and then joined into a tube.

Heels

There are two heel-shaping styles used in crocheting the socks in this book: heel flaps with gusset shaping and short-rowed heels.

The heel flap with gusset shaping consists of a rectangular flap that comes down around the back of the heel. The section at the bottom of the heel is called the heel turn. The heel turn is crocheted with decreases to shape the heel at the bottom so that it cups under the heel of your foot. A gusset section incorporates the heel flap into the sock foot by adding stitches along the side edges of the heel. Crocheting stitches together where the heel meets the front of the foot creates a triangular wedge, decreasing the gusset section to fit the foot. This is one area where stitch markers are very helpful (see "Working with Markers," page 10).

A short-rowed heel is made using a stair-step method that results in a heel that is similar to the heel of a commercial sock. Decreases are made by leaving stitches unworked at the end of each row. This creates little steps going up the sides of the heel. Stitches are then worked into these unworked stitches, one row at a time, to increase the heel back to the required number of stitches. You may want to place stitch markers in the unworked stitches to use as a guide for where to work the stitches.

Note: You may find that when you work a short-rowed heel, you will get a small hole or gap at one side where the heel meets the foot front. This is usually caused by the last turning row. To eliminate this, work an additional slip stitch into the foot front on the next-to-the-last row of the heel. When working the first round of the foot front (or the leg on toe-up socks), decrease the extra slip stitch by working it with the first stitch on the heel to keep your stitch count correct.

Before you begin the heel on a sock worked from the toe up, fold the sock flat with the toe centered and positioned correctly on your sock so that your heel will be centered on the back of the foot.

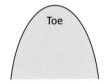

Fold toe-up sock flat to center and position toe correctly.

When working stitches along the side edges of the heel, insert the hook through a portion of the stitch while being careful not to split the yarn. Do not insert your hook around the post of a stitch or the space between rows, as this will make an edge that looks sloppy and it will leave holes.

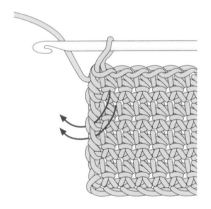

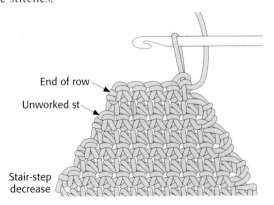

Short-Rowed Heel Decreases

Toe Shaping

To create a nearly invisible beginning for socks worked from the toe up, slip stitch into the bottom loop (or hump) of the beginning chain. Work your slip stitches the same size as the beginning chain stitches. This is a foundation row that closes and neatens up the toe and it is not counted as the first round of the toe.

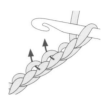

Then to begin the first round of the toe, pivot your work and begin working in the top loops of the actual chain. Work your first single crochet stitch of round 1 in the first chain that was made.

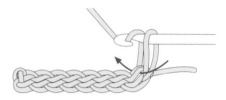

Continue to work single crochet stitches along the chain, pivot the work, and single crochet in each slip stitch of the foundation row.

When working in the round, your work will naturally spiral unless you keep the decreases or increases at the side edges. Place markers at each end of the piece to mark the side edges of the toe, which will keep increases positioned correctly for shaping the toe. Move the markers with each round to keep them at the side edges of the foot. This may or may not be at the same decrease or increase of the round just completed. It may be one or two stitches to either side (see "Working with Markers" on page 10). If the toe stitches spiral into the foot, you will have an uncomfortable and poorly fitting sock.

Making Custom-Fitted Socks

If you can measure the foot, first follow the directions in "Taking Measurements" on page 9 to take the measurements of the foot. Once you have the measurements, you will turn to the section "Finished Dimensions" in the sock pattern and refer to the circumference measurements for either the leg or the foot to determine which size sock to make. For top-down socks, follow the pattern directions based on the measurement for the leg circumference; you'll want to find the measurement that most closely matches your measurement and follow the corresponding directions for the entire sock. For toe-up socks, follow the pattern directions based on the measurement for the foot circumference; you'll need to find the measurement that most closely matches your measurement and follow the corresponding directions for the entire sock. Exceptions to these rules are noted in the patterns Ribbed Hiker and Red Hot. If possible, we suggest that you try the sock on often while making it so that you can make sure the sock fits. In most of the patterns you can make adjustments to the leg and/or foot circumference without disrupting the pattern stitch by decreasing or increasing one or two stitches.

If you cannot measure the foot, ask the recipient of the sock for his or her shoe width (narrow, medium, wide, extra wide) and shoe size. Refer to the shoe width chart on page 8 to determine the approximate foot circumference measurements. For both top-down and toe-up socks, match the chart measurement as closely as possible with one of the foot circumference measurements in the pattern (see section "Finished Dimensions" in pattern) and follow the corresponding directions for the entire sock. Listed after the shoe width chart is the shoe size chart, which you can use to determine the approximate finished length of the sock foot from heel to toe. You'll need this information when you are crocheting the foot of the sock. Note that the finished length of the sock foot is generally ¼" to ¾" shorter than the actual length of the person's foot.

Pattern Sizing

The measurements listed in the following charts are based on standardized measurements for men's and women's shoe widths and shoe sizes.

Shoe Width

(Approximate Foot Circumference at Ball of Foot (B on Diagram, Page 9)

Women				
Shoe Width	Narrow	Medium	Wide	Extra Wide
Approx. Foot Circumference	6¾" to 7¼"	7½" to 8½"	9" to 9½"	9¾" to 11¼"
Men				
Shoe Width	Narrow	Medium	Wide	Extra Wide
Approx. Foot Circumference	8½" to 8¾"	9" to 10"	10½" to 11"	12" to 13"

Shoe Size

Women's Shoe Size (Standard American)	Measurement of Actual Foot	Finished Length of Sock Foot
4 to 4½	8⅜"	7¾" to 8"
5 to 5½	8¾"	8¼" to 8½"
6 to 6½	9"	8½" to 8¾"
7 to 7½	9⅜"	9" to 9¼"
8 to 8½	9¾"	9¼" to 9½"
9 to 9½	10"	9½" to 9¾"
10 to 10½	10⅜"	10" to 10¼"
11 to 11½	10¾"	10¼" to 10½"

Men's Shoe Size (Standard American)	Measurement of Actual Foot	Finished Length of Sock Foot
8 to 9	10" to 10½"	9½" to 10"
10 to 11	10½" to 11"	10" to 10½"
12 to 13	11¼" to 11¾"	10½" to 11¼"
14	12"	11¼" to 11½"

Taking Measurements

Take measurements, as shown, of your foot or the person's foot you plan to crochet socks for.

A. While standing, measure up the leg from the floor to the height of the sock listed in the pattern. At this point, measure the circumference of the actual leg to determine the circumference of the sock leg.

B. Measure the circumference of foot at B, around the ball of the foot. The finished sock should be about ½" to ¾" narrower than the measurement for B.

C. While standing, measure the foot from the back of the heel to the longest toe for the length of foot (heel to toe). The finished foot length should be ¾" to 1" shorter than the measurement for C.

D. For toe-up socks, while standing, measure the foot from the longest toe to just below the ankle to determine where to begin the heel.

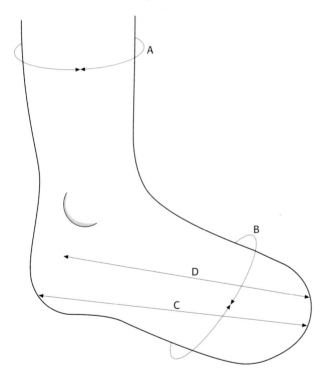

Calculating Your Gauge

To make sure your socks match the measurements given in the patterns, take the time to make a gauge swatch. When working in the round, your gauge will be slightly different than working back and forth; we recommend that you work your swatch in the round.

Make a chain of 24 stitches and slip stitch into the first chain to form a circle. Make sure you do not twist the chain. Work the leg pattern for 10 rows. Measure the circumference of the swatch. Divide the 24 stitches by the circumference measurement for the number of stitches per inch. Measure the length of the swatch. Divide the 10 rows by the length measurement for the number of rows per inch.

If you have more stitches per inch than the required gauge, try a larger hook. If you have fewer stitches per inch, try a smaller hook. If your stitches match but your rows are slightly off, it's usually a matter of correcting your tension. If you have less rows than listed in the pattern, tighten up your tension. If you have more rows, loosen up a bit.

If your foot pattern is different than your leg pattern, you may want to work a separate swatch for the foot.

Special Instructions and Stitches

In this section you'll learn more about crochet techniques, such as working with multiple colors and markers, as well as detailed how-to instructions for a variety of stitches.

Changing Colors

To change colors, drop old color to wrong side of work. Then work the last 2 loops off the hook with the new color.

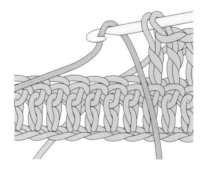

Working with Multiple Colors

Do not cut the yarn unless stated in the instructions. Carry unused color on the wrong side, bringing it up to the next row by crocheting under the unused yarn in the first stitch of each new row or round.

Working with Markers

The pattern instructions will tell you to place a marker (PM) in a specific stitch or area of the sock to mark the beginning of a round or areas to increase or decrease. For increasing and decreasing, the pattern will instruct you to work up to a specific number of stitches prior to or at the marker. Here's an example: "sc to 3 sts prior to marker." Locate the marker and count back 3 stitches, excluding the stitch with the marker. Then work the 3 stitches as stated in the directions.

Special Crochet Stitches

Use the following special crochet stitches to create more elastic-like cuff edges, unique textures, and interesting patterns.

Double Crochet Foundation (dcf)

By starting the cuff of a sock with the double crochet foundation, you end up with an edge that is more elastic than an edge started with a traditional chain. Ch 3. YO, insert hook into third ch from hook. YO, pull yarn through st.

YO, pull yarn through 1 lp on hook (ch 1 made).

YO, pull yarn through 2 lps on hook.

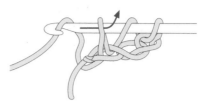

YO, pull yarn through last 2 lps on hook (first dc made). *YO, insert hook through fl and bottom hump of the ch.

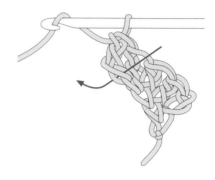

YO, pull yarn through, ch 1, YO, pull yarn through 2 lps on hook, YO, pull yarn through last 2 lps on hook*, rep from * to *, making each new dc in the previous ch.

Front-Post Double Crochet (FPDC)

YO, insert hook from front to back around indicated dc post, YO, pull yarn through, (YO, pull yarn through 2 lps) 2 times. Always sk st in back of FPDC unless otherwise directed.

Back-Post Double Crochet (BPDC)

YO, insert hook from back to front around indicated dc post, YO, pull yarn through, (YO, pull yarn through 2 lps) 2 times. Always sk st in back of BPDC unless otherwise directed.

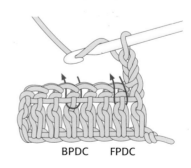

BPDC   FPDC

Crossed Cable Pattern

The crossed cable pattern is used in Harlequin Cables. Sk 2 sts, dc in next st, ch 1, FPDC around dc below first skipped st 2 rnds below. Do not work the FPDC around the previous post st.

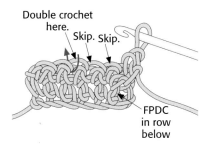

Extended Single Crochet (esc)

Insert hook into next st, YO, pull yarn through st, YO, pull yarn through 1 lp on hook.

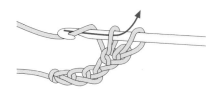

YO, pull yarn through 2 lps on hook.

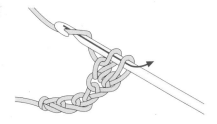

Long Single Crochet (lsc)

Insert hook between specified sts 2 or more rows (or rnds) below. Hook is not inserted into the post of the st. It is actually worked between 2 sts. YO, pull yarn through st, YO, pull yarn through 2 lps on hook.

Split Single Crochet (ssc)

Insert hook into post (or V) of sc in previous row (or round), YO, pull yarn through st, YO, pull yarn through 2 lps on hook.

Long Split Single Crochet (lssc)

Insert hook into post (or V) of previous ssc 2 rows (or rounds) below, YO, pull yarn through st, YO, pull yarn through 2 lps on hook.

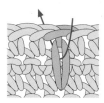

Reverse Single Crochet (rsc)

Working from left to right, insert hook into st to right of hook, YO, pull yarn through st, YO, pull yarn through 2 lps on hook.

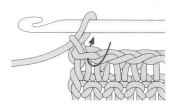

Increasing and Decreasing (inc and dec)

When inc, work 2 sts into 1 st. When dec, work over 2 sts.

Single Crochet Decrease (sc2tog)

Insert hook into next st, YO, pull yarn through st, insert hook into next st, YO, pull yarn through st, YO, pull yarn through all lps on hook.

Half Double Crochet Decrease (hdc2tog)

YO, insert hook into next st, YO, pull yarn through st, insert hook into next st, YO, pull yarn through st, YO, pull yarn through all lps on hook.

Double Crochet Decrease (dc2tog)

YO, insert hook into next st, YO, pull yarn through st, YO, pull yarn through 2 lps, YO, insert hook into next st, YO, pull yarn through st, YO, pull yarn through 2 lps, YO, pull yarn through all lps on hook.

Slip Stitch Decrease (slst2tog)

Insert hook into next st, YO, pull yarn through st, insert hook into next st, YO, pull yarn through all lps on hook.

Finishing

Once you complete your socks, the last thing you want is to have a sloppy closure at the toe or along the side of the cuff or leg. The toes should have a nice, neat finish. One of the best methods for achieving this is to use a mattress seam or invisible seam when sewing the toe closed or seaming up a sideways cuff and leg.

Sewing the Toe

Fold the sock flat with the heel centered at the back of the foot.

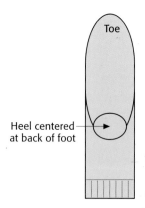

Sock Folded Flat

With the right sides of the sock facing out, align the stitches on the front and the back of the toe. With a large blunt needle and matching yarn, insert the needle under the post between 2 stitches and pull the needle through. Go under the post between 2 stitches on the opposite side and pull the needle through. Work from one side of the toe to the other side of the toe.

Pull up thread every 3 or 4 stitches to close the stitched portion of the toe. Continue in this manner along the edge to be sewn.

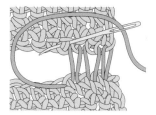

Sewing the Cuff or Leg

Align the side edges of the cuff (or leg) with the right sides facing out. With a large blunt needle and matching yarn, insert the needle under the front loop on one side edge of the cuff (or leg), and then under the back loop on the opposite side edge of the cuff (or leg). Pull the needle and yarn through. Continue in this manner along the edge to be sewn.

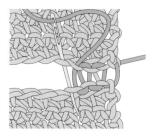

Care and Handling

The following tips will help keep crocheted socks looking their best. Crocheted socks are special and unique, so care should be taken when putting them on and laundering them.

Trying on Socks

When trying socks on, ease them gradually onto your foot like a nylon stocking—do not pull them on from the cuffs. Crocheted socks are not as elastic as knit socks. The socks will stretch a little after working with them and checking them for fit. Occasionally squeeze your socks gently together in your hands to restore their shape.

Washing Tips

Wash your socks following the yarn label instructions. If using a washing machine, turn your socks inside out and place them in a lingerie bag or use sock minders (see page 5). If you find that your wool or cotton socks feel harsh, use fabric softener or a capful of hair conditioner in the final rinse cycle to soften them up. Shape and lay the socks flat to dry.

Abbreviations

approx	approximately		lssc	long split single crochet
beg	begin(ning)		MC	main color
bl	back loop		pat	pattern
BPDC	back-post double crochet		PM	place marker
ch	chain		rem	remaining
ch sp	chain space		rep	repeat
cir	circumference		rnd(s)	round(s)
cont	continue(ing)		RS	right side
dc	double crochet		rsc	reverse single crochet
dcf	double crochet foundation		sc	single crochet
dc2tog	double crochet 2 together		sc2tog	single crochet 2 together
dec	decrease(ing)		sk	skip
esc	extended single crochet		sl st	slip stitch
fl	front loop		slst2tog	slip stitch 2 together
FPDC	front-post double crochet		sp	space
hdc	half double crochet		ssc	split single crochet
hdc2tog	half double crochet 2 together		st(s)	stitch(es)
inc	increase(ing)		tog	together
incl	including		WS	wrong side
lps	loop(s)		YO	yarn over
lsc	long single crochet			

Come rain or shine, your fabulous crocheted socks will get the attention they deserve in these chic, clear plastic boots designed especially to show off fashionably clad feet.

EASY DOES IT

By Janet Rehfeldt

Easy Does It is just that—easy to crochet for a great basic sock. This would be a good pattern for your first pair of crocheted socks because it will familiarize you with the basic sock structure. The simple stitch pattern used throughout the leg and foot makes this the perfect sock for use with self-striping yarns. Socks with a narrow foot will have wider stripes of color than socks with a wide foot, but the striping will still be apparent on the wider sock leg and foot. Note that you need to begin each of your socks with the same color sequence or your socks will not match. Also, if you must add yarn while in the middle of your project, begin with the yarn color that you left off with to continue the same color pattern.

Featured Techniques

This pattern features the top-down method, the foundation stitch cuff, and the heel flap with gusset.

Featured Stitches

Back-post double crochet (BPDC); page 10

Chain (ch)

Double crochet foundation (dcf); page 10

Extended single crochet (esc); page 11

Front-post double crochet (FPDC); page 10

Long split single crochet (lssc); page 11

Single crochet (sc)

Single crochet decrease (sc2tog); page 11

Slip stitch (sl st)

Materials

- 2 (2, 3, 3) balls Lana Grossa Meilenweit Cotton Fun (45% cotton, 42% wool, 13% nylon; 50 g, 190 m per ball), color 331
- Size D (3.25 mm) hook for leg and foot (or size required to obtain gauge)
- Size E (3.5 mm) for cuff
- 3 stitch markers

Finished Dimensions
(WITH SOCK FOLDED FLAT)

Cir of leg (unstretched): 7¼ (8, 8¾, 9¼)"

Cir of foot (unstretched): 7¼ (8, 8¾, 9¼)"

Floor to cuff: 8½"

Gauge

6 sts and 6 rnds = 1" with size D hook

Note: Unless otherwise instructed, do not sl st rnds closed, and do not ch 1 at beg of rnds and rows.

Cuff

Foundation rnd: With size E hook, ch 3, work 43 (47, 51, 55) dcf, sl st in top of beg ch 3 to close rnd (beg ch 3 counts as first dc). [44 (48, 52, 56) dc]

Rnd 1: *FPDC around next dc, BPDC around next dc*, rep from * to * around.

Rnd 2: *FPDC around next FPDC, BPDC around next BPDC*, rep from * to * around.

Rep rnd 2 another 2 times. On last rnd, sl st in first dc of rnd.

EASY DOES IT

Leg

Rnd 1: Sc in each st around. [44 (48, 52, 56) st]

Rnd 2: Esc in each sc around.

Rep rnds 1 and 2, change to size D hook on rnd 6, and work until 5½" from beg, incl cuff, end with rnd 2. Do not fasten off.

Heel

Row 1 (RS): Sc in next 25 (25, 27, 27) sts, turn, rem sts unworked.

Row 2: Ch 1, sc in first sc and each sc across, turn.

Row 3: Ch 1, sc in first sc, *lssc in sc 2 rows below, sc in next sc*, rep from * to * across, turn.

Row 4: Ch 1, sc first sc and each sc across, turn.

Row 5: Ch 1, sc in first sc, *lssc in lssc 2 rows below, sc in next sc*, rep from * to * across, turn.

Rep rows 4 and 5 until heel measures 2¾" to 3", end with a RS row.

Heel Turn

Row 1 (WS): Ch 1, sc in first sc, sc2tog twice, sc in next 5 (5, 6, 6) sc, sc2tog twice, sc in next 6 (6, 7, 7) sc, sc2tog twice, sc in last sc, turn. [19 (19, 21, 21) sc]

Row 2: Ch 1, sc in first sc, sc2tog twice, sc in next 2 (2, 3, 3) sc, sc2tog twice, sc in next 3 (3, 4, 4) sc, sc2tog twice, sc in last sc, turn. [13 (13, 15, 15) sc]

Rows 3: Ch 1, sc in first sc, sc2tog, sc to last 3 sc, sc2tog, sc in last sc, turn. [11 (11, 13, 13) sc]

Row 4: Ch 1, sc in first sc, sc2tog, sc to last 3 sc, sc2tog, sc in last sc. Do not turn. [9 (9, 11,11) sc]

Gusset

Rnd 1 (RS): Work 18 sc sts evenly along right edge of heel flap, PM, sc across 19 (23, 25, 29) front foot sts, work 18 sc sts evenly along left side edge of heel flap, PM in first sc on left side of heel, sc in 9 (9, 11,11) heel sts, PM in last sc made to mark beg of rnds. [64 (68, 72, 76) sc]

Rnd 2: Esc in each sc around foot. [64 (68, 72, 76) esc]

Rnd 3: Sc to 3 sts prior to first marker at gusset, sc2tog twice, sc across foot front to next gusset marker, sc2tog twice, sc in rem heel sts. [60 (64, 68, 72) sc]

Rep rnds 2 and 3 until 44 (48, 52, 56) sc rem, end with rnd 3. Remove gusset markers.

Foot

Rnd 1: Esc in each sc around. [44 (48, 52, 56) esc]

Rnd 2: Sc in each esc around.

Rep rnds 1 and 2 until foot measures 2" from longest toe, end with rnd 2.

Shape Toe

PM at each side edge. Move markers after each rnd to keep them at side edges of sock.

Rnd 1: Sc to 2 sts prior to first marker, sc2tog, sc in next st, sc2tog, sc to 2 sts prior to next marker, sc2tog, sc in next st, sc2tog (this is partial rnd to set up toe). [40 (44, 48, 52) sc]

Rnd 2: Sc to 2 sts prior to first marker, sc2tog, sc in next st, sc2tog, sc to 2 sts prior to next marker, sc2tog, sc in next st, sc2tog. [36 (40, 44, 48) sc]

Rep rnd 2 until 16 (20, 20, 24) sts rem. Fasten off. Sew toe.

Featured Techniques

This pattern features the top-down method, the sideways slip-stitch cuff, the short-rowed heel, and shaped arch.

Featured Stitches

Chain (ch)

Double crochet (dc)

Single crochet (sc)

Single crochet decrease (sc2tog); page 11

Slip stitch (sl st)

Materials

MC: 2 (2, 2, 2, 3, 3, 3) balls Lana Grossa Meilenweit (80% virgin wool, 20% nylon; 50 g, 200 m per ball), color Light Gray #1102

CC: 1 ball Lana Grossa Meilenweit, color Dark Gray #1104

Size D (3.25 mm) hook (or size required to obtain gauge)

3 stitch markers

For alternate colorway:

MC: 2 (2, 2, 3, 3, 3, 3) balls Lana Grossa Meilenweit Cotton (45% cotton, 42% wool, 13% nylon; 50 g, 109 m per ball), color Light Tan #24

CC: 1 ball Lana Grossa Meilenweit Cotton, color Medium Tan #18

Finished Dimensions
(WITH SOCK FOLDED FLAT)

Cir of leg (unstretched): 7½ (8½, 9, 9½, 10, 10¾, 11½)"

Cir of foot (unstretched): 7 (8, 8½, 9, 9½, 10¼, 10¾)"

Floor to cuff: 7" to 9"

Gauge

6.5 sts and 5.75 rnds = 1"

Note: Unless otherwise instructed, do not sl st rnds closed, and do not ch 1 at beg of rnds and rows.

Cuff

Row 1: With MC, ch 10, sl st in second ch from hook, *sl st in bl of next ch, rep from * across, turn. [9 sl st]

Row 2: Ch 1, sl st in bl of first sl st and in each st across, turn. [9 sl st]

Rep row 2 for 78 (82, 86, 90, 94, 98, 102) rows total. Bring short ends of cuff tog, matching row 78 (82, 86, 90, 94, 98, 102) to row 1, sl st in base of first row to close. Sew cuff closed (see page 12). Working along bottom long edge of cuff, work 50 (54, 58, 62, 66, 70, 74) sc evenly spaced.

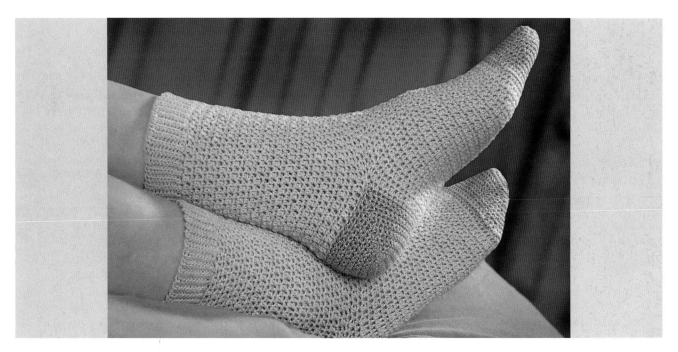

Leg

Rnd 1: *Sc in next st, dc in next st, rep from * around. PM for beg of rnd. Move marker with each rnd. [50 (54, 58, 62, 66, 70, 74) sts]

Rnd 2: Sc in each st around.

Rnd 3: *Dc in next st, sc in next st, rep from * around.

Rnd 4: Sc in each st around.

Rep rnds 1–4 for pat st until sock measures 6" to 7" from beg incl cuff, end with rnd 3. Do not fasten off MC.

Heel

Row 1 (RS): With CC, sc in first st, PM, sc in 24 (26, 29, 30, 32, 34, 36) sts, PM, turn. Rem sts unworked. [25 (27, 29, 31, 33, 35, 37) sc]

Row 2: Sc in first sc and each sc across, leave last sc unworked, turn. [24 (26, 28, 30, 32, 34, 36) sc]

Rep row 2 until 9 (9, 11, 11, 11, 13, 13) sts rem, turn.

Heel Increase

Row 1 (WS): Sc in 9 (9, 11, 11, 11, 13, 13) sc, sc in closest unworked st down side of heel, sc in next unworked st down side of heel, sl st in side edge of heel, turn. [11 (11, 13, 13, 13, 15, 15) sc]

Row 2: Sk sl st, sc in 11 (11, 13, 13, 13, 15, 15) sc, sc in closest unworked st down side of heel, sc in next unworked st down side of heel, sl st in side edge of heel, turn. [13 (13, 15, 15, 15, 17, 17) sc]

Row 3: Sk sl st, sc in 13 (13, 15, 15, 15, 17, 17) sc, sc in next unworked st down side of heel, sl st in side edge of heel, turn. [14 (14, 16, 16, 16, 18, 18) sc]

Rep row 3, inc 1 st on each row until you have 23 (25, 27, 29, 31, 33, 35) sc along heel.

Next row: Sk sl st, sc in 23 (25, 27, 29, 31, 33, 35) sc, sc in next unworked st down side of heel, sl st in side edge in first row at base of heel, turn. [24 (26, 28, 30, 32, 34, 36) sc]

Next row: Sk sl st, sc in 24 (26, 28, 30, 32, 34, 36) sc, sc in next unworked st down side of heel, sl st in side edge in first row at base of heel. Do not turn. Fasten off CC. [25 (27, 29, 31, 33, 35, 37) sc]

Foot

Rnd 1 (RS): Pick up MC, sc in each st around foot. PM to mark beg of rnds. Move marker with each rnd. [50 (54, 58, 62, 66, 70, 74) sc]

Work as for leg rep in pat (rnds 1–4) until foot measures 1½" from heel, end with rnd 1 or 3 of pat.

Shape Arch

Next rnd: Working in a sc rnd of pat st, dec 4 sts evenly spaced around foot by sc2tog. [46 (50, 54, 58, 62, 66, 70) sc]

Cont in pat st until foot measures 2½" from longest toe, end with rnd 1 or 3 of pat.

Shape Toe

PM at each side edge of foot. Move markers with each rnd to keep them at side edges of foot.

Rnd 1: Work in sc to center back of foot. Change to CC (do not fasten off MC). Work 1 rnd sc in CC. Do not fasten off. [46 (50, 54, 58, 62, 66, 70) sc]

Rnd 2: With MC, sc to 2 sts prior to first marker, sc2tog, sc in next sc, sc2tog, sc to 2 sts prior to next marker, sc2tog, sc in next sc, sc2tog, sc to center back of foot, fasten off MC, bringing up CC. [42 (46, 50, 54, 58, 62, 66) sc]

Rnd 3: With CC, sc to 2 sts prior to first marker, sc2tog, sc in next sc, sc2tog, sc to 2 sts prior to next marker, sc2tog, sc in next sc, sc2tog, sc to center back of foot. [38 (42, 46, 50, 54, 58, 62) sc]

Rnd 4: Sc in each sc around.

Rnds 5–6: Rep rnds 3 and 4 one more time. [34 (38, 42, 46, 50, 54, 58) sc]

Rep rnd 3 until 22 (22, 22, 26, 26, 26, 28) sts rem. Fasten off, weave in ends.

Fancy Cuffs

By Mary Jane Wood

Fancy Cuffs is a great sock if you want to try crocheting from the toe up. This easy pattern stitch, which only looks difficult, produces a very stretchy and elegant-looking sock. The shell cluster cuff gives Fancy Cuffs a graceful style. The sock is best suited to a wool-blend yarn.

Featured Techniques

This pattern features the toe-up method and short-rowed heel.

Featured Stitches

Back-post double crochet (BPDC); page 10

Chain (ch)

Double crochet (dc)

Front-post double crochet (FPDC); page 10

Half double crochet (hdc)

Single crochet (sc)

Slip stitch (sl st)

Materials

A: 2 (2, 2, 3) balls Schoeller Esslinger Fortissima (75% wool, 25% nylon; 50 g, 210 m per ball), color 73 Blue

B: 20 yds Schoeller Esslinger Fortissima in Off-White for cuffs

Size E (3.5 mm) hook (or size required to obtain gauge)

Finished Dimensions
(WITH SOCK FOLDED FLAT)

Cir of leg (unstretched): 6 (7, 7½, 8½)"

Cir of foot (unstretched): 6 (7, 7½, 8½)"

Floor to cuff: Approx 7"

Gauge

2 shells = 1"

13 hdc = 2"

Pattern Stitches

Shell: (Sc, ch 1, 2 hdc) in same stitch.

FPDC Cluster: (YO, insert hook from front to back around post of next dc, YO, pull up a lp, YO, pull through 2 lps) 5 times, YO, pull through all 6 lps on hook.

Note: Unless otherwise instructed, do not sl st rnds closed, and do not ch 1 at beg of rnds and rows.

Toe

Foundation row: With A, ch 13 (16, 18, 20), sl st in bottom lp of second ch from hook, sl st in next 10 (13, 15, 17) ch, 2 hdc in last ch. [13, 16, 18, 20) sts]

Rnd 1: Pivot work to work in top lps of beg ch, hdc in each of next 11 (14, 16, 18) ch, 2 hdc in next ch; pivot work, hdc in each sl st of foundation row. PM at each end to mark side edges of foot. Move markers after each rnd to keep increases at side edges of toe. [26 (32, 36, 40) hdc]

Rnd 2: *Hdc in each st to next marker, 2 hdc in next st*, rep from * to * once more. [28 (34, 38, 42) hdc]

Rep rnd 2 until you have 36 (42, 46, 50) sts.

Foot

Rnd 1: (Shell in next st, sk 2 sts) 12 (14, 15, 16) times, (shell in next st, sk 1 st) 0 (0, 0, 1) time. [12 (14, 15, 17) shells]

Rnd 2: *Shell in next ch 1 sp, rep from * around.

Rep rnd 2 until foot reaches just below anklebone, or approx 2½" shorter than length of foot from heel to toe.

Heel

Fold sock to position toe correctly on foot (see page 6).

Row 1 (RS): Cont in pat until you reach side edge of sock, (sc in next sc, sk ch sp, sc in next 2 hdc) 6 (7, 7, 8) times, sc in next 1 (1, 1, 0) sc, sc in next ch sp 1 (0, 0, 0) times, leave rem sts unworked, turn. [20 (22, 22, 24) sc]

Row 2: Sc in first sc and each sc of heel, leaving last st unworked, turn. [19 (21, 21, 23) sc]

Rows 3–15: Rep row 2, working 1 less st in each row. [6 (8, 8, 10) sc at end of row 15]

Row 16 (WS): Sc in each sc in row 15, sc in closest unworked st down side of heel, sc in side edge of next row, sl st in next unworked st, turn. [8 (10, 10, 12) sc]

Row 17: Sk sl st, sc in each sc in row 16, sc in closest unworked st down side of heel, sc in side edge of next row, sl st in next unworked st, turn. [10 (12, 12, 14) sc]

Row 18: Sk sl st, sc in each sc in last row, sc in next closest unworked st down side of heel, sl st in side of next row, turn. [11 (13, 13, 15) sc]

Rows 19-25: Rep row 18, working 1 more st in each row. [18 (20, 20, 22) sc at end of row 25]

Row 26: Sk sl st, sc in each st in last row, sc in next closest unworked st, sl st in next st on front of foot, turn. [19 (21, 21, 23) sts]

Row 27: Sk sl st, sc in each st in last row, sc in next closest unworked st, sl st in first st on front of foot. [20 (22, 22, 24) sc]. Do not fasten off. Do not turn.

Leg

Rnd 1(RS): Working along front of foot, (shell in ch-1 sp of next shell) 6 (7, 8, 9) times, working along sc of heel, (sk first st, shell in next st, sk 2 sts) 6 (7, 7, 8) times, sl st in first st to close rnd. [12 (14, 15, 17) shells]

Rnd 2: *Shell in next ch-1 sp, rep from * around.

Rep rnd 2 in pat until leg measures approx 3¾" from top of heel.

Next rnd: *Sc in next sc, sk ch-1 sp, sc in each of next 2 hdc*, rep from * to * around. [36 (42, 45, 51) sc]. Do not fasten off A.

Clustered Shell Cuff

 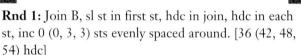 Note: Work all ch sts loosely.

Rnd 1: Join B, sl st in first st, hdc in join, hdc in each st, inc 0 (0, 3, 3) sts evenly spaced around. [36 (42, 48, 54) hdc]

Rnd 2: With A, sc in each hdc around.

Rnd 3: With B, ch 4 (counts as first dc and 1 ch), sk 2 sts, 5 dc in next st, ch 1, (sk 2 sts, dc in next st, ch 1, sk 2 sts, 5 dc in next st, ch 1) 5 (6, 7, 8) times, sk rem sts, sl st in third ch of beg ch 4 to close rnd.

Rnd 4: FPDC around beg ch 4, ch 2, work FPDC Cluster over next 5 sts, *ch 2, FPDC around next dc, ch 2, work FPDC Cluster over next 5 sts*, rep from * to * around, ch 2, sl st in first st to close rnd.

Rnd 5: With A, *sc in next FPDC, 2 sc in next ch-2 sp, sc in next cluster, 2 sc in next ch-2 sp*, rep from * to * around. Fasten off A.

Rnd 6: Join B, ch 1, hdc in each st around.

Rnd 7: *Ch 3, working in bottom lp of ch, work 3 (2, 3, 2) dc in third ch from hook, sk next 3 (2, 3, 2) sts, sl st in next st*, rep from * to * around. Fasten off.

TUTTI-FRUTTI

By Janet Rehfeldt

The use of slip stitches for this sock allows you to create stitches that look like knit and purl stitches. This crochet method is often referred to as "poor man's knitting." Crocheters tend to work slip stitches tighter than regular crochet stitches because they are commonly used for neatening or tightening up the work. Check your gauge often when working with a slip-stitch pattern for socks. You want your stitches to remain constant and to match the gauge.

Featured Techniques

This pattern features the top-down method, the sideways single crochet cuff, and the heel flap with gusset.

Featured Stitches

Back loop (bl)

Chain (ch)

Single crochet (sc)

Single crochet decrease (sc2tog); page 11

Slip stitch (sl st)

Special Stitch

Slip stitch 2 together (slst2tog): Insert hook into bl of next sl st, YO, pull through lp, insert hook into bl of next sl st, YO, pull through all lps on hook (dec made).

Materials

2 (2, 3, 3) balls Lana Grossa Meilenweit Cotton Fun (45% cotton, 42% wool, 13% nylon; 50 g, 190 m per ball), color 5271

Size D (3.25 mm) hook for cuff and heel

Size G (4.25 mm) hook for leg, gusset, and foot (or size required to obtain gauge)

3 stitch markers

Finished Dimensions
(WITH SOCK FOLDED FLAT)

Cir of leg (unstretched): 7¾ (8, 8½, 9)"

Cir of foot (unstretched): 7¾ (8, 8½, 9)"

Floor to cuff: 8"

Gauge

6.25 sts and 9.25 rnds = 1" in sl st pat with size G hook

Note: Unless otherwise instructed, do not sl st rnds closed, and do not ch 1 at beg of rnds and rows.

Cuff

Row 1: With size D hook, ch 9, sc in bl of second ch from hook, sc in bl of each ch across, turn. [8 sc]

Rows 2–54 (58, 60, 64): Ch 1, sc in bl of each sc across, turn.

Leg

Foundation row: Work 48 (52, 56, 60) sc sts evenly along long edge of work, sl st in first sc to close rnd. Sew cuff closed (see page 12).

Rnd 1 (WS): Sl st in bl of first sc, sl st in bl of each sc around. [48 (52, 56, 60) sl sts]

Rnd 2: Change to size G hook. Sl st in bl of each sl st around.

Rep rnd 2 until leg measures 5" from beg incl cuff. Do not fasten off. Turn to RS of work.

Heel

Row 1 (RS): Change to size D hook. Sc in next 24 (24, 26, 26) sl sts, turn. Rem sts unworked.

Row 2: Ch 1, sc first sc and each sc across, turn.

Rep row 2 until heel measures 2¾", end on a WS row.

Heel Turn

Row 1 (RS): Ch 1, sc in first sc, *sc2tog twice, sc in each of next 5 (5, 6, 6) sc*, rep from * to * once, sc2tog twice, sc in last sc, turn. [18 (18, 20, 20) sc]

Row 2: Ch 1, sc in first sc, *sc2tog twice, sc in each of next 2 (2, 3, 3) sc*, rep from * to * once, sc2tog twice, sc in last sc, turn. [12 (12, 14, 14) sc]

Row 3: Ch 1, sc in first sc, sc2tog, sc to last 3 sc, sc2tog, sc in last sc, turn. [10 (10, 12, 12) sc]

Row 4: Rep row 3. Do not turn. [8 (8, 10, 10) sc]

Gusset

Worked on WS of work.

Rnd 1 (WS): Work 18 sc evenly along right edge of heel flap, PM, sl st in bl in each sl st across foot front, work 18 sc evenly along left side edge of heel flap, PM in first sc of left side of heel, sc in 8 (8, 10, 10) heel sts, PM to mark beg of rnd; move markers with each rnd. [68 (72, 76, 80) sc]

Rnd 2: Change to size G hook, sl st in bl of each sc to 1 st prior to first marker at gusset, slst2tog, sl st in bl across foot front to next gusset marker, slst2tog, sl st in bl of rem heel sts. [66 (70, 74, 78) sl sts]

Rnd 3: Work even.

Rnd 4: Sl st in bl of each sl st to 1 st prior to first marker at gusset, slst2tog, sl st in bl across foot front to next gusset marker, slst2tog, sl st in bl of rem heel sts. [64 (68, 72, 76) sl sts]

Rep rnds 3 and 4 until 48 (52, 56, 60) sl sts rem. Remove gusset markers.

Foot

Cont as for leg in est sl st pat, working in bl, until foot measures 2" from longest toe.

Shape Toe

PM at each side edge. Move markers after each rnd to keep them at side edges of sock.

Rnd 1: Work to 2 st prior to first marker, slst2tog, sl st in bl of next sc, slst2tog, sl st in bl to 2 sts prior to next marker, slst2tog, sl st in bl of next sc, slst2tog. [44 (48, 52, 56) sc]

Repeat rnd 1 until 20 sts rem.

Turn sock RS out. Fasten off. Sew toe.

CONFETTI

By Janet Rehfeldt

The trendy rolled cuff on this sock is a terrific fashion statement. The cuff begins with a basic chain. Unlike a foundation-stitch beginning, this chain will not have the flexibility or give that the foundation stitch has. Therefore, it is important to crochet your beginning chain loose but not sloppy. You may want to use one hook size larger on the beginning chain, and then change to the specified hook in the pattern for the remaining rounds of the cuff.

Featured Techniques

This pattern features the top-down method, the rolled cuff, and the heel flap with gusset.

Featured Stitches

Back loop (bl)

Chain (ch)

Double crochet (dc)

Front-post double crochet (FPDC); page 10

Half double crochet (hdc)

Single crochet (sc)

Single crochet decrease (sc2tog); page 11

Slip stitch (sl st)

Materials

Short Cuff

2 (2, 2, 3) balls Zitron Trekking Color (75% wool, 25% nylon; 50 g, 210 m per ball), color 41

Long Cuff

2 (2, 3, 3) balls Schachenmayr Regia plus Cotton Color (38% wool, 37% cotton, 25% nylon; 50 g, 225 m per ball), color 86

Both Versions

Size D (3.25 mm) hook for leg, heel, and foot (or size required to obtain gauge)

Size E (3.5 mm) hook for cuff

3 stitch markers

Finished Dimensions
(WITH SOCK FOLDED FLAT)

Cir of leg (unstretched): 7½ (8, 8¾, 9½)"

Cir of foot (unstretched): 7½ (8, 8¾, 9½)"

Floor to cuff: 6" or 8" with cuff rolled

Gauge

5.25 sts and 4 rnds = 1" in hdc with size D (3.25 mm) hook

6.25 sts and 7 rnds = 1" in foot pat with size D (3.25 mm) hook

Note: Unless otherwise instructed, do not sl st rnds closed, and do not ch 1 at beg of rnds and rows.

Cuff

Rnd 1: With size E hook, ch 40 (44, 48, 52). Working in bl of ch, sc in second ch from hook, sl st in next ch, *sc in next ch, sl st in next ch*, rep from * to * across. [39 (43, 47, 51) sts]

Rnd 2: Being careful not to twist work, sl st in first sc of prev rnd, PM to mark beg of rnd. Sc in next st, *sl st in next sc, sc in next sl st*, rep from * to * around.

Rnd 3: *Sc in next sl st, sl st in next sc*, rep from * to * around.

Rnd 4: *Sl st in next sc, sc in next sl st*, rep from * to * around.

Rep rnds 3 and 4 until cuff measures 2" from beg; cuff will naturally roll onto itself.

Leg

Rnd 1: *Hdc in bl of next st, hdc in next st*, rep from * to * around. [39 (43, 47, 51) sts]

Rnd 2: Change to size D hook. *Hdc in next st, hdc in bl next st*, rep from * to * around.

Rep rnd 2 until leg measures 4½" for short leg or 6½" for longer leg from beg incl cuff. Do not fasten off.

Heel

Row 1 (RS): Sc in next 19 (21, 23, 25) sts, turn. Rem sts unworked.

Row 2: Ch 1, sc in first sc and each sc across, turn.

Row 3: Ch 1, sc in first 2 sc, *FPDC around next sc 2 rows below, sc in next sc*, rep from * to * across, sc in last sc, turn.

Row 4: Ch 1, sc in first sc and each sc across, turn.

Row 5: Ch 1, sc in first 2 sc, *FPDC around FPDC 2 rows below, sc in next sc*, rep from * to * across, sc in last sc, turn.

Rep rows 4 and 5 until heel measures 2¾", end on a RS row.

Heel Turn

Row 1 (WS): Ch 1, sc in first sc, sc2tog twice, sc in next 3 (4, 4, 5) sc, sc2tog twice, sc in next 2 (3, 5, 6) sc, sc2tog twice, sc in last sc, turn. [13 (15, 17, 19) sc]

Row 2: Ch 1, sc in first 5 (7, 7, 8) sc, sc2tog, sc in last 5 (6, 8, 9) sc, turn. [12 (14, 16, 18) sc]

Row 3: Ch 1, sc in first sc, sc2tog, sc to last 3 sc, sc2tog, sc in last sc, turn. [10 (12, 14, 16) sc]

Row 4: Ch 1, sc in first sc, sc2tog, *sc in next 1 (2, 3, 4) sc, sc2tog*, rep from * to * once, sc in last sc. Do not turn. [7 (9, 11, 13) sc]

Gusset

Rnd 1 (RS): Work 19 sc sts evenly along right edge of heel flap, PM in last sc, dc in first st on foot front, *sc in next st, dc in next st*, rep from * to * across rem 17 (19, 21, 23) front foot sts, work 20 sc evenly along left side edge of heel flap, PM in first sc on left side of heel, sc in 7 (9, 11, 13) heel sts, PM in last sc to mark beg of rnds. [66 (70, 74, 78) sc]

Rnd 2: Sc to 3 sts prior to first marker at gusset, sc2tog twice, sc across foot front to next gusset marker, sc2tog twice, sc in rem heel sts. [62 (66, 70, 74) sc]

Rnd 3: *Sc in next sc, dc in next sc*, rep from * to * around foot.

Rep rnds 2 and 3 until 46 (50, 54, 58) sts rem, end with rnd 2. Remove gusset markers.

Foot

Rnd 1: *Sc in next sc, dc in next sc*, rep from * to * around foot. [46 (50, 54, 58) sts]

Rnd 2: Sc in each st around foot.

Rep rnds 1 and 2 until foot measures 2" from longest toe, end with rnd 2.

Shape Toe

PM at each side edge. Move markers after each rnd to keep them at side edges of sock.

Rnd 1: Sc to 2 sts prior to first marker, sc2tog, sc in next st, sc2tog, sc to 2 sts prior to next marker, sc2tog, sc in next st, sc2tog (partial rnd to set up toe). [42 (46, 50, 54) sc]

Rnd 2: Sc to 2 sts prior to first marker, sc2tog, sc in next st, sc2tog, sc to 2 sts prior to next marker, sc2tog, sc in next st, sc2tog. [38 (42, 46, 50) sc]

Rep rnd 2 until 18 (22, 22, 22) sts rem. Fasten off. Sew toe.

TENNIS ANYONE?

By Janet Rehfeldt

These socks are just the thing for the tennis court or a walk in the park. Working with elasticized yarn is quite different from working with yarns that have no stretch or give to them. Your sock should be sized so that it fits snug but comfortable. Work the foot length 1" to 1½" shorter than your actual foot length and ¼" to ½" smaller than your foot circumference. Don't pull the yarn tight as you crochet your stitches. Allow the yarn to stretch just slightly so that it remains flexible and allows your sock to stretch to fit your foot.

Featured Techniques

This pattern features the top-down method, the foundation stitch cuff, and the heel flap with gusset.

Featured Stitches

Chain (ch)

Back-post double crochet (BPDC); page 10

Double crochet (dc)

Double crochet foundation (dcf); page 10

Front-post double crochet (FPDC); page 10

Single crochet (sc)

Single crochet decrease (sc2tog); page 11

Slip stitch (sl st)

Materials

2 (2, 2, 2) balls Cascade Fixation (98.3% cotton, 1.7% elastic; 50 g, 186 yds stretched and 100 yds relaxed per ball), color 8001 White

1 ball Cascade Fixation, color 2550 Lapis Blue

Size E (3.5 mm) hook (or size required to obtain gauge)

3 stitch markers

Finished Dimensions
(WITH SOCK FOLDED FLAT)

Cir of leg (unstretched): 6¾ (7¼, 8, 8¾)"

Cir of foot (unstretched): 6¾ (7¼, 8, 8¾)"

Floor to cuff: 4"

Gauge

6.25 sts and 5.75 rnds = 1"

> Note: Unless otherwise instructed, do not sl st rnds closed, and do not ch 1 at beg of rnds and rows. Work FPDC and BPDC in row below unless otherwise instructed.

Cuff

Foundation rnd: With blue, ch 3, work 41 (45, 49, 53) dcf, sl st in top of beg ch 3 to close rnd (beg ch 3 counts as first dc). Change to white. [42 (46, 50, 54) sts]

Rnd 1: *FPDC around next dc, BPDC around next dc*, rep from * to * around.

Rnd 2: *FPDC around next FPDC, BPDC around next BPDC*, rep from * to * around.

Rnds 3 and 4: Rep rnd 2. At end of rnd 4, sl st in first st. Change to blue.

TENNIS ANYONE?

Heel

Row 1 (RS): Sc in first dc, sc in next 22 (22, 24, 24) sts, turn. [23 (23, 25, 25) sc]. Rem 19 (23, 25, 29) sts unworked.

Row 2: Ch 1, sc in first sc and each sc across, turn.

Row 3: Ch 1, sc in first sc, *FPDC around next FPDC 3 rows below, sc in next sc*, rep from * to * across, turn.

Row 4: Ch 1, sc in first sc and each sc across, turn.

Row 5: Ch 1, sc in first sc, *FPDC around next FPDC 2 rows below, sc in next sc*, rep from * to * across, turn.

Rep rows 4 and 5 until heel measures 2½ (2½, 2½, 2¾)", end on RS row.

Heel Turn

Row 1 (WS): Ch 1, sc in first sc, sc2tog twice, sc in next 5 (5, 6, 6) sc, sc2tog, sc in next 6 (6, 7, 7) sc, sc2tog twice, sc in last sc, turn. [18 (18, 20, 20) sc]

Row 2: Ch 1, sc in first sc, sc2tog twice, sc in next 8 (8, 10, 10) sc, sc2tog twice, sc in last sc, turn. [14 (14, 16, 16) sc]

Row 3: Ch 1, sc in first sc, sc2tog twice, sc to last 5 sc, sc2tog twice, sc in last sc, turn. [10 (10, 12, 12) sc]

Row 4: Ch 1, sc in first sc, sc2tog, sc to last 3 sts, sc2tog, sc in last sc, turn. [8 (8, 10, 10) sc]

Row 5: Ch 1, sc in first sc, sc2tog, sc to last 3 sts, sc2tog, sc in last sc, turn. [6 (6, 8, 8) sc] Change to white.

Gusset

Do not close rnds with sl st unless otherwise instructed. Do not ch 1 at beg of rnds.

Rnd 1 (RS): Sc in 6 (6, 8, 8) heel sts, work 16 (16, 18, 18) sc sts evenly along right edge of heel flap, PM, sc across 18 (22, 24, 28) front foot sts, 2 sc in next st, work 16 (16, 18, 18) sc sts evenly along left side edge of heel flap, PM in first sc on left side of heel, PM in last sc made to mark beg of rnd. [58 (62, 70, 74) sts]

Rnd 2: Sc to 3 sts prior to marker at gusset, sc2tog twice, sc across foot front to next gusset marker, sc2tog twice, sc in rem heel sts. [54 (58, 66, 70) sc]

Rnd 3: *Dc in next sc, sc in next sc*, rep from * to * around.

Rep rnds 2 and 3 until 42 (46, 50, 54) sts rem, end with rnd 3. Remove gusset markers.

Foot

Rnd 1: *Dc in next sc, sc in next sc*, rep from * to * around. [42 (46, 50, 54) sts]

Rnd 2: Sc in each st around.

Rep rnds 1 and 2 in pat until foot measures 2½" to 2¾" from longest toe, end with rnd 2.

Next rnd: Change to blue, sl st in each sc around.

Shape Toe

PM at each side edge. Move markers after each rnd to keep them at side edges of sock.

Rnd 1: Change to white, work in white sts only behind blue sts, sc to 2 sts prior to first marker, sc2tog, sc in next st, sc2tog, sc to 2 sts prior to next marker, sc2tog, sc in next st, sc2tog (partial rnd to set up toe). [38 (42, 46, 50) sc]

Rnd 2: Sc to 2 sts prior to first marker, sc2tog, sc in next st, sc2tog, sc to 2 sts prior to next marker, sc2tog, sc in next st, sc2tog. [34 (38, 42, 46) sc]

Rep rnd 2 until 14 (14, 18, 18) sts rem.

Fasten off. Sew toe.

RIBBED HIKER

By Janet Rehfeldt

Using a split single crochet in the round gives you the look and feel of a knit stockinette stitch. Work your split stitches so that they are slightly loose or you will have a hard time working into the stitch on the following round and you might split or rip the yarn. As long as you meet the gauge requirements, this boot or hiking sock has the stretch and fit of a knit sock. Ribbing on the leg will give up to 3" and the foot will give up to 1½", allowing the widest width to fit a foot with a 13" circumference. The pattern is written in seven leg and foot widths. You'll want to make socks for yourself and for your hiking buddies too!

Featured Techniques

This pattern features the top-down method, the foundation stitch cuff, and the heel flap with gusset.

Featured Stitches

Back-post double crochet (BPDC); page 10

Chain (ch)

Double crochet foundation (dcf); page 10

Front-post double crochet (FPDC); page 10

Single crochet (sc)

Single crochet decrease (sc2tog); page 11

Slip stitch (sl st)

Split single crochet (ssc); page 11

Materials

2 (3, 3, 3, 4, 4, 4) skeins Brown Sheep Wildfoote (85% wool, 15% nylon; 50 g, 215 yds per skein), color SY-08 Geranium

Size E (3.5 mm) hook for cuff and leg (or size required to obtain gauge)

Size G (4.0 mm) hook for heel and foot

3 stitch markers

Finished Dimensions
(WITH SOCK FOLDED FLAT)

Due to the stretch in the leg pattern, we recommend that you follow the pattern directions for the measurement that most closely matches your foot circumference.

Cir of leg (unstretched): 6½ (7¼, 8, 8¾, 9½, 10¼, 10¾)"

Cir of foot (unstretched): 7 (7½, 8⅓, 9¼, 9⅝, 10⅔, 11⅓)"

Floor to cuff: 7½" to 9¾"

Gauge

5.25 sts and 7 rnds = 1" with size G hook in ssc

> Note: Unless otherwise instructed, do not sl st rnds closed, and do not ch 1 at beg of rnds and rows.

Cuff and Leg

Foundation rnd: With size E hook, ch 3, work 47 (50, 53, 56, 59, 62, 65) dcf, sl st in top of beg ch 3 to close rnd (beg ch 3 counts as first dc). [48 (51, 54, 57, 60, 63, 66) dc]

Rnd 1: *FPDC around each of next 2 dc, BPDC around each of next dc*, rep from * to * around.

Rnd 2: *FPDC around each of next 2 FPDC, BPDC around each of next BPDC*, rep from * to * around.

Rep rnd 2 until leg measures 5" to 7" from beg, depending on choice for length of cuff.

Heel Flap

Row 1: Ch 1, sc in each of next 22 (22, 22, 24, 24, 26, 26) sts, turn. Rem sts unworked.

Row 2: Ch 1, sc in first sc and each sc across, turn.

Rep row 2 until heel flap measures 2½" to 2¾".

Heel Turn

Row 1 (RS): Ch 1, sc in first sc, *sc2tog twice, sc in each of next 4 (4, 4, 5, 5, 6, 6) sc*, rep from * to * one more time, sc2tog twice, sc in last sc, turn. [16 (16, 16, 18, 18, 20, 20) sc]

Row 2: Ch 1, sc in first sc and each sc across, turn.

Row 3: Ch 1, sc in first sc, sc2tog 1 (1, 1, 2, 2, 2, 2) times, sc in each of next 10 (10, 10, 8, 8, 10, 10) sts, sc2tog 1 (1, 1, 2, 2, 2, 2) times, sc in last sc, turn. [14 (14, 14, 14, 14, 16, 16) sc]

Row 4: Ch 1, sc in first sc and each sc across, turn.

Row 5: Ch 1, sc in first sc, sc2tog, sc to last 3 sc, sc2tog, sc in last sc, turn. [12 (12, 12, 12, 12, 14, 14) sc]

Row 6: Ch 1, sc in each of first 4 (4, 4, 4, 4, 5, 5) sc, sc2tog twice, sc in each of last 4 (4, 4, 4, 4, 5, 5) sc, turn. [10 (10, 10, 10, 10, 12, 12) sc]

Row 7: Ch 1, sc in first sc and each sc across. Do not turn. Do not fasten off.

Gusset

> Note: When working split single crochet stitches, pull up your loop to the height of the current row and work stitches so that they are slightly loose.

Rnd 1: Change to size G hook, work 14 (14, 15, 16, 17, 18, 18) sc evenly spaced along edge of heel flap, PM, sc in each of 26 (29, 32, 33, 36, 37, 40) front foot sts, work 14 (15, 15, 17, 17, 17, 18) sc evenly spaced along top edge of heel flap, PM in first sc to mark beg of gusset, sc in each of 10 (10, 10, 10, 10, 12, 12) sts along top of heel, PM to mark beg of rnds. [64 (68, 72, 76, 80, 84, 88) sc]

Rnd 2: Ssc to 3 sts prior to first gusset marker, sc2tog twice, ssc in each sc across foot front, sc2tog twice, ssc in rem sts. [60 (64, 68, 72, 76, 80, 84) sts]

Rnd 3: Ssc in each st around.

Rnds 4–11: Rep rnds 2 and 3 another 4 times. [44 (48, 52, 56, 60, 64, 68) ssc at end of rnd 11]

Rnd 12 and 13: Rep rnd 2. [36 (40, 44, 48, 52, 56, 60) sts at end of rnd 13.]

Foot

Cont in ssc around foot until sock measures 2½" from longest toe.

Shape Toe

PM at each side edge. Move markers after each round to keep at side edges of sock. There will be 36 (40, 44, 48, 52, 56, 60) sts when you start the toe shaping. Follow directions for your size according to the number of sts listed below.

For 36 (40, 44) sts

Rnd 1: Ssc to first marker, sc2tog, ssc in each st to next marker, sc2tog, ssc in each st to first marker (partial rnd to set up toe). [34, (38, 42) sts]

Rnd 2: Ssc to first marker, sc2tog, ssc in each st to next marker, sc2tog. [32 (36, 40) sts]

Rep rnd 2 until 20 sts rem.

For 48 (52, 56, 60) sts

Rnd 1: Ssc to 2 sts prior to first marker, sc2tog twice, ssc in each st to 2 sts prior to next marker, sc2tog twice (partial rnd to set up toe). [44, (48, 52, 56) sts]

Rnds 2–4: Ssc to first marker, sc2tog twice, ssc in each st to next marker, sc2tog twice. [32 (36, 40, 44) sts at end of rnd 4]

Rnd 5: Ssc to first marker, sc2tog, ssc in each st to next marker, sc2tog. [30 (34, 38, 42) sts]

Rep rnd 5 until 24 (24, 26, 26) sts rem.

All Sizes

Ssc 1 rnd even without dec. Fasten off. Sew toe.

PEBBLED SAND

By Janet Rehfeldt

Subtle tone-on-tone yarn combined with a pebbled texture make this beautiful sock a perfect match for slacks or jeans. The texture is achieved by working a long single crochet between stitches two rounds below.

Featured Techniques

This pattern features the toe-up method, the short-rowed heel, and the ribbed cuff.

Featured Stitches

Chain (ch)

Double crochet (dc)

Extended single crochet (esc); page 11

Front-post double crochet (FPDC); page 10

Long single crochet (lsc); page 11

Single crochet (sc)

Slip stitch (sl st)

Materials

2 (2, 3, 3) balls Schachenmayr Regia Color (75% wool, 25% nylon; 50 g, 210 m per ball), color F1900

Size E (3.5 mm) hook (or size required to obtain gauge)

3 stitch markers

Finished Dimensions
(WITH SOCK FOLDED FLAT)

Cir of leg (unstretched): 7 (7¾, 8½, 9)"

Cir of foot (unstretched): 6¾ (7¼, 8, 8¾)"

Floor to cuff: 7¾"

Gauge

5.25 sts and 7.5 rnds = 1"

 Note: Unless otherwise instructed, do not sl st rnds closed, and do not ch 1 at beg of rnds and rows.

Toe

Foundation row: Ch 10, working in bottom lp, sl st in second ch from hook, sl st in each ch. [9 sl st]

Rnd 1: Working in top lps of beg ch, sc in each ch, pivot work, sc in each sl st of foundation row [18 sc]. PM at each end to mark side edges of toe. Move markers with each rnd to keep markers at side edges of toe.

Rnd 2: *Sc to 1 st prior to marker, 2 sc in next sc, 1 sc in marked st, 2 sc in next sc*, rep from * to * once. [22 sc]

Rnd 3: *Sc to 1 st prior to marker, 2 sc in next sc, 1 sc in marked st, 2 sc in next sc*, rep from * to * once. [26 sc]

Rnd 4: Work even around.

Rep rnds 3 and 4 until 34 (38, 42, 46) sc rem. Remove markers.

Foot

Work lsc between the sc and lsc 2 rnds below, sk sc directly behind lsc. Do not work into the actual leg or post of st.

Rnd 1: Esc in each st around. PM to mark beg of rnd. Move marker with each rnd. [34 (38, 42, 46) esc]

Rnd 2: *Sc in next esc, lsc between next 2 sc 2 rows below*, rep from * to * around.

Rnd 3: Esc in each st around.

Rnd 4: *Sc in next esc, lsc between sc and lsc 2 rnds below*, rep from * to * around.

Rep rnds 3 and 4 until foot reaches just below anklebone, end with rnd 4. Do not fasten off.

Heel

Fold sock to position toe correctly on foot (see page 6). Work to a side edge.

Row 1 (RS): Sc in first 22 (22, 24, 24) sc, turn. Rem sts unworked.

Row 2: Sc in first sc and each sc across, turn.

Row 3: Sc in first sc and each sc across, leaving last sc unworked, turn. [21 (21, 23, 23) sc]

Rep row 3 until 9 (9, 11, 11) sts rem, turn.

Heel Increase

Row 1 (WS): Sc in 9 (9, 11, 11) sc, sc in side edge of heel, sc in closest unworked st down side of heel, sl st in side edge of heel, turn. [11 (11, 13, 13) sc]

Row 2: Sk sl st, sc in 11 (11, 13, 13) sc, sc in side edge of heel, sc in closest unworked st down side of heel, sl st in side edge of heel, turn. [13 (13, 15, 15) sc]

Row 3: Sk sl st, sc in 13 (13, 15, 15) sc, sc in next unworked st down side of heel pulling st close to last sc made, sl st in side edge of heel, turn. [14 (14, 16, 16) sc]

Rows 4–10: Rep row 3, inc 1 st in each row, turn. [20 (20, 22, 22) sc at end of row 10]

Row 11: Sk sl st, sc in 20 (20, 22, 22) sc, sc in next unworked st down side of heel, sl st in side edge of heel, turn. [21 (21, 23, 23) sc]

Row 12: Sk sl st, sc in 21 (21, 23, 23) sc, sc in next unworked st down side of heel, sl st in side edge of heel. Do not turn. [22 (22, 24, 24) sc]

Leg

Work lsc between the sc and lsc 2 rnds below, sk sc directly behind lsc. Do not work into the actual leg or post of st.

Rnd 1 (RS): Esc in each st around foot and heel, working 1 sc in last sl st on each side of heel. PM to mark beg of rnd. Move marker with each rnd. [36 (40, 44, 48) esc]

Rnd 2: Work rnd 4 of foot pat across foot front, sc in each esc around heel.

Rnd 3: Esc in each st around.

Rnd 4: Work rnd 4 of foot pat across foot front, cont pat around heel, work lsc sts between sc sts in rnd 2 of leg.

Rnd 5: Esc in each st around.

Rnd 6: *Sc in next esc, lsc between sc and lsc 2 rnds below, sk sc st directly behind lsc just made*, rep from * to * around.

Rep rnds 5 and 6 until leg measures 5" from beg, end with rnd 6, sl st in first sc to close rnd.

Cuff

Rnd 1: Dc in each st around. [36 (40, 44, 48) dc]

Rnd 2: *FPDC around next dc, dc in next dc*, rep from * to * around.

Rnd 3: *FPDC around next FPDC, dc in next dc*, rep from * to * around.

Rep rnd 3 once, working rnd slightly looser to fit leg. Fasten off.

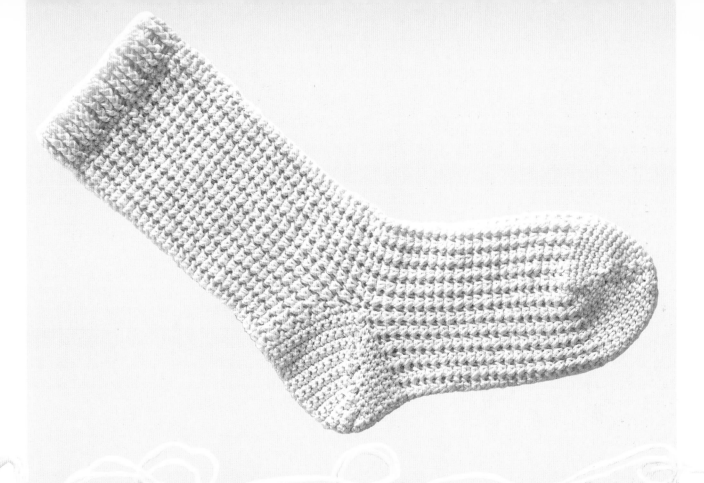

MINICLUSTERED LACE

By Janet Rehfeldt

Lace patterns tend to have more give or stretch than most solid patterns used in socks, and this makes them nicely suited for cotton yarns, which are not considered very stretchy. When worked correctly, the lace pattern in Miniclustered Lace should align straight up and down along your leg and foot. The small cluster pattern looks similar to a knitted lace pattern and is slightly stretchy.

Featured Techniques

This pattern features the top-down method, the foundation stitch cuff, and the short-rowed heel.

Featured Stitches

Back-post double crochet (BPDC); page 10

Chain (ch)

Double crochet (dc)

Double crochet foundation (dcf); page 10

Front-post double crochet (FPDC); page 10

Single crochet (sc)

Single crochet decrease (sc2tog); page 11

Slip stitch (sl st)

Materials

2 balls Schoeller Esslinger Fortissima Cottolaua, (38% wool, 37% cotton, 25% nylon; 50 g, 210 m per ball), color 10 Cream

Size E (3.5 mm) hook (or size required to obtain gauge)

16 stitch markers

Finished Dimensions
(WITH SOCK FOLDED FLAT)

Cir of leg (unstretched): 7 (7¼, 7½, 8)"

Cir of foot (unstretched): 7 (7¼, 7½, 8)"

Floor to cuff: 9½"

Gauge

3.25 clusters and 5 rnds = 1"

Note: Unless otherwise instructed, do not sl st rnds closed, and do not ch 1 at beg of rnds and rows.

Cuff

Foundation rnd: Ch 3, work 39 (43, 47, 51) dcf, sl st in top of beg ch 3 to close rnd (beg ch 3 counts as first dc). [40 (44, 48, 52) dc]

Rnd 1: *FPDC around each of next 3 dc, BPDC around next dc*, rep from * to * around.

Rnd 2: *FPDC around each of next 3 FPDC, BPDC around next FPDC*, rep from * to * around.

Rep rnd 2 another 3 times. On last rnd, sl st in first dc of rnd.

Leg

Note: Each minicluster should align directly over the top of minicluster in row below. Your work should not spiral around the leg.

Rnd 1: Sc in each st around, inc 6 (4, 2, 0) sts evenly on cuff. [46 (48, 50, 52) sc]

Rnd 2: Work Minicluster pat as follows: *Insert hook into next sc, YO, pull up a lp, insert hook into next sc, YO, pull up a lp, YO, pull through 3 lps on hook, ch 1 (cluster made)*, rep from * to * around, sl st in top of cluster in this rnd only. PM for beg of rnds. Move marker with each rnd. [23 (24, 25, 26) miniclusters]

Rnd 3: *Insert hook into ch sp, YO, pull up a lp, insert hook into st at top of cluster, YO, pull up a lp, YO, pull through 3 lps on hook, ch 1*, rep from * to * around.

Rep rnd 3 in pat until leg measures 7" from beg incl cuff. Do not fasten off.

Heel

Row 1 (RS): *Sc in ch sp, sc in top of minicluster*, rep from * to * until 22 (22, 22, 24) sc rem, turn. Rem 12 (13, 14, 14) miniclusters unworked.

Row 2: Ch 1, sc in first sc and each sc across, turn.

Row 3: Sc in first sc and each sc across, leaving last sc unworked, turn. [21 (21, 21, 23) sts]

Rep row 3 until 7 (7, 7, 9) sts rem, turn.

Heel Increase

Row 1 (WS): Sc in 7 (7, 7, 9) sc, sc in side edge of heel, sc in closest unworked st down side of heel, sl st in side edge of heel, turn. [9 (9, 9, 11) sc]

Row 2: Sk sl st, sc in 9 (9, 9, 11) sc, sc in side edge of heel, sc in closest unworked st down side of heel, sl st in side edge of heel, turn. [11 (11, 11, 13) sc]

Row 3: Sk sl st, sc in 11 (11, 11, 13) sc, sc in next closest unworked st down side of heel pulling st close to last sc made, sl st in side edge of heel, turn. [12 (12, 12, 14) sc]

Rows 4–10: Rep row 3, inc 1 st on each row, turn. [19 (19, 19, 21) sc at end of row 10]

Row 11: Sk sl st, sc in 19 (19, 19, 21) sc, sc in next closest unworked st down side of heel pulling st close to last sc made, sl st in side edge of heel, turn. [20 (20, 20, 22) sc]

Row 12: Sk sl st, sc in 20 (20, 20, 22) sc, sc in next closest unworked st down side of heel pulling st close to last sc made, sc in side edge of heel. Do not turn. [22 (22, 22, 24) sc]

Foot

PM in first minicluster st, move marker with each rnd.

Rnd 1 (RS): Work minicluster in each st around front part of foot. *Insert hook into next sc, YO, pull up a lp, insert hook into next sc, YO, pull up a lp, YO, pull through 3 lps on hook, ch 1*, rep from * to * across heel sts. [23 (24, 25, 26) miniclusters]

Rep rnd 3 of leg pat until foot measures 2" from longest toe.

Toe Decrease

PM at each side edge. If you are not at a marker, work to next marker. Move markers after each rnd to keep markers at side edges of sock.

Rnd 1: Sc in each ch st and st at the top of each minicluster around. [46 (48, 50, 52) sc]

Rnd 2: Sc2tog, sc to side marker, sc2tog (partial rnd to set up toe). [44, (46, 48, 50) sc]

Rnds 3–5: Sc to first marker, sc2tog, sc to next marker, sc2tog. [38 (40, 42, 44) sc at end of rnd 5]

Rnd 6: Sc to 1 st before first marker, sc2tog twice, sc to 1 st before next marker, sc2tog twice.

Rep rnd 6 until 18 (20, 22, 24) sc rem.

Fasten off. Sew toe.

JACQUARD! JACQUARD!

By Janet Rehfeldt

There are some fantastic yarns on the market now that are dyed to create a Fair Isle or Jacquard pattern without having to work the stitches with separate colors and strands of yarn. As shown in Jacquard! Jacquard!, alternating a minishell pattern consisting of single crochet stitches with a round of single crochet retains the color pattern that the yarn was intended to have. Note that you need to begin each of your socks with the same color sequence or your socks will not match. Also, if you must add yarn while in the middle of your project, begin with the yarn color that you left off with to continue the same color pattern.

Rnd 2: With A, ch 3, working in bl dc in each st around, sl st with B in top of beg ch 3.

Rnd 3: With B, dc in fl of next st 2 rnds below, sc in each of next 3 sts, *dc in fl of next st 2 rnds below, sc in each of next 3 sts*, rep from * to * around, sl st with A in bl of first st.

Rnd 4: Rep rnd 2.

Rnd 5: With B, sc in top of first ch and in next st, *dc in fl of next st 2 rnds below, sc in each of next 3 sts*, rep from * to * around to last 2 sts, dc in fl of next st 2 rnds below, sc in next st, sl st with A in bl of first st.

Rep rnds 2–5 another 3 (4, 4, 4) times.

Last rnd: Rep rnd 2.

Heel

Row 1 (RS): With B, working over A, dc in fl of next st 2 rows below, sc in each of next 3 sts, *dc in next fl of next st 2 rows below, sc in each of next 3 sts*, rep from * to * 2 (3, 3, 4) more times, rem sts unworked, turn. [16 (20, 20, 24) sts]

Row 2: Ch 1, sc in first st and each st across, turn.

Rep row 2 until heel measures 2¾" to 3", end with an even row.

Heel Turn

Row 1: Ch 1, *sc2tog twice, sc in next 2 (4, 4, 6) sts*, rep from * to * once, sc2tog twice, turn. [10 (14, 14, 18) sc]

Row 2: Ch 1, sc in first sc and each sc across, turn.

Row 3: Ch 1, sc in next 3 (5, 5, 7) sts, sc2tog twice, sc in last 3 (5, 5, 7) sts, turn. [8 (12, 12, 16) sc]

Rows 4–5: Rep row 2, omitting turn on row 5. Do not fasten off.

Gusset

Rnd 1 (RS): Work 14 sc evenly spaced along right edge of heel, working in front leg sts, dc in fl of next st 2 rnds below, PM in this st to mark gusset and beg of rnd, sc in next 3 sts, *dc in fl of next st 2 rnds below, sc in next 3 sts*, rep from * to * 3 (3, 4, 4) more times.

Working in left side edge of heel, work 14 sc evenly spaced, finish off B. Move marker with each rnd. [56 (60, 64, 68) sts incl sts along top of heel]

Rnd 2: Attach A in marked st, (esc in next st, dc in next st) 10 (10, 12, 12) times along foot front, sc2tog, dc2tog, (esc in next st, dc in next st) around to 4 sts prior to marker, sc2tog, dc2tog. [52 (56, 60, 64) sts]

Rnd 3: (Dc in next esc, esc in next dc) 10 (10, 12, 12) times along foot front, dc2tog, sc2tog, (dc in next st, esc in next st) around to 4 sts prior to marker, dc2tog, sc2tog. [48 (52, 56, 60) sts]

Rnd 4: (Esc in next dc, dc in next esc) 10 (10, 12, 12) times along foot front, sc2tog, dc2tog, (esc in next st, dc in next st) around to 4 sts prior to marker, sc2tog, dc2tog. [44 (48, 52, 56) sts]

Rep rnds 3–4 until you have 36 (40, 44, 48) sts. Keep beg rnd marker.

Foot

Rnd 1: *Dc in next esc, esc in next dc*, rep from * to * around.

Rnd 2: *Esc in next dc, dc in next esc*, rep from * to * around.

Rep rnds 1 and 2 until foot measures 2" from longest toe, end with rnd starting with an esc.

Toe Decrease

Rnd 1: PM at left edge of sock in esc, PM on right edge of sock in esc, *(dc in next esc, esc in next dc), rep between ( ) until you reach next marker, dc2tog, sc2tog*, rep from * to * once, work even in pat to end of rnd, esc in last st. [32 (36, 40, 44) sts]

Rnd 2: Move markers at both edges to a dc, *(esc in next st, dc in next st), rep between ( ) until you reach next marker, sc2tog, dc2tog*, rep from * to * once, work even to end of rnd, dc in last st. [28 (32, 36, 40) sts]

Rep rnds 1 and 2 once, then rep rnd 1 once, or until sock just reaches your longest toe. Fasten off. Sew toe.

TERRIFIC THONG

By Mary Jane Wood

Terrific Thong, with its separate large toe, is just the ticket for thongs and split-toe sandals. This pattern works up fast into medium-weight, super comfortable socks. Spikes of color are made by working stitches in skipped stitches two rows down. The color changes are easy to do, and the contrasting dark and light multicolored yarn on the leg remind me of little city lights seen from a distance.

Featured Techniques

This pattern features the top-down method, the sideways slip stitch cuff, and the short-rowed heel.

Featured Stitches

Chain (ch)

Extended single crochet (esc); page 11

Single crochet (sc)

Single crochet decrease (sc2tog); page 11

Slip stitch (sl st)

Materials

A: 1 ball Cascade 220 (100% wool; 100 g, 220 yds), color 4009 Teal

B: 1 ball Cascade 220 Quatro, color 9432 Variegated Green-Blue

Size F (3.75 mm) hook (or size required to obtain gauge) for cuff

Size G (4.25 mm) hook for leg and foot

Finished Dimensions
(WITH SOCK FOLDED FLAT)

Cir of leg (unstretched): 7¼ (8½, 9¾, 11)"

Cir of foot (unstretched): 7 (8, 9, 10¼)"

Floor to cuff: Approx 9"

Gauge

Leg: 3.29 sts and 3 rows = 1" in leg pat st with size G hook

Foot: 3.50 sts and 3.75 rows = 1" in foot pat st with size G hook

Special Stitch

Esc2tog: Insert hook in next st, YO, pull up lp, insert hook into next st, YO, pull up lp, YO, and pull through all lps (1 st dec).

 Note: Unless otherwise instructed, do not sl st rnds closed, and do not ch 1 at beg of rnds and rows.

Cuff

Row 1: With A and size F hook, leaving a long tail, ch 5, sl st in second ch from hook and in bottom lp of each ch st, turn. [4 sl st]

Row 2: Ch 1, sl st in bl of each st, turn. [4 sl st]

Rep row 2 another 47 (55, 63, 71) times.

Bring short ends of cuff tog, matching row 48 (56, 64, 72) to row 1, sl st in base of first row to close. Working in end of rows, ch 1, sc in edge of every other row around, sl st in first st, change to B. Sew cuff closed (see page 12). Do not fasten off. [24 (28, 32, 36) sc]

Leg

Change to size G hook. PM to mark beg of each rnd. Move marker with each rnd.

Rnd 1: With B, sl st in first st, *2 esc in next st, sk next st*, rep from * to * around. [24 (28, 32, 36) esc]

Rnd 2: With A, *sk next st, sc in next st, esc in skipped st below*, rep from * to * around.

Rnd 3: With A, esc in each st around, changing to B on last st.

Rep rnds 1–3 until leg measures about 6¾" from beg of cuff, end with rnd 3.

Last rnd: Sc in each st around, sl st in first st, cut yarn.

Heel

Row 1 (RS): Fold sock so sl st join runs down middle. Hold sock upside down, attach A with sc on right side edge, sc in each of next 11 (13, 15, 17) sts, leaving 12 (14, 16, 18) sts unworked, turn. [12 (14, 16, 18) sc]

Row 2: Ch 1, sc in first st and each st across, turn.

Row 3: Sc in each st of heel, leaving last st unworked, turn. [11 (13, 15, 17) sc]

Rows 4–10: Rep row 3, working 1 less st each rnd. [4 (6, 8, 10) sc at end of row 10]

Row 11: Sc in 4 (6, 8, 10) sc, sc in closest unworked st down side of heel, sc in side edge of heel, sl st in next unworked st, turn. [6 (8, 10, 12) sc]

Row 12: Sk sl st, sc in 6 (8, 10, 12) sc, sc in closest unworked st down side of heel, sc in side edge of heel, sl st in next unworked st, turn. [8 (10, 12, 14) sc]

Rows 13 and 14: Sk sl st, sc in each sc in last row, sc in closest unworked st down side of heel, turn. [10 (12, 14, 16) sc at end of row 14]

Rows 15 and 16: Sc in each sc, sc in closest unworked st, insert hook in edge of row 1 of heel, YO and pull up a lp, insert hook in next unworked st on front of foot, YO and pull up a lp, YO and pull through all 3 lps, sl st in next st on front of foot, turn. [14 (16, 18, 20) sc at end of row 16]

Foot

Rnd 1 (RS): With A, sk sl st, sc in next 14 (16, 18, 20) sts along heel, change to B in last st, sc in sl st, sc in next 8 (10, 12, 14) sts along front of foot, sc in sl st, finish off A. [24 (28, 32, 36) sc]

Rnd 2: With B from now on, esc in each st around.

Rnd 3: Sc in each st around.

Rep rnds 2 and 3 until foot measures 1" less than desired length. Finish off.

Big Toe for Right Sock

Rnd 1 (RS): With bottom of foot facing you, attach yarn with a sc at right edge, sc in each of next 3 (4, 5, 6) sts, ch 4, turn sock to top of foot, working from left to right, count 4 (5, 6, 7) sts from left side edge, sc in this st at top of foot. Working from right to left, sc in 3 (4, 5, 6) sts. [8 (10, 12, 14) sc and 4 ch]

Rnd 2: Esc in each st and in each ch. [12 (14, 16, 18) esc]. Adjust number of ch sts, if necessary, to fit toe.

Work even in est foot pat (rep rnds 2 and 3 of foot) until piece is ¼" less than toe, finishing with an esc rnd.

Next rnd: Sc2tog around.

Rep last rnd until 4 sts rem. Sew up toe.

Remainder of Toe Area for Right Sock

Rnd 1 (RS): With bottom of foot facing you, working right to left, sc in first free st to left of big toe, sc in next 15 (17, 19, 21) sts, working into bottom of ch 4, sc in each ch st. [20 (22, 24, 26) sc]

Rnd 2: With bottom of foot facing you, PM on left edge, esc in each st to marker, esc2tog in marked st, esc in rem sts, replace marker. [19 (21, 23, 25) esc]

Rnd 3: Sc in each st up to marker, sc2tog in marked st, sc in rem sts, replace marker. [18 (20, 22, 24) sc]

Rep rnds 2 and 3 until sock is ⅛" less than longest toe.

Last rnd: Cont in pat st, dec 1 st on each edge.

Fasten off. Sew toe area.

Toe Shaping for Left Sock

Follow "Big Toe for Right Sock" and "Remainder of Toe Area for Right Sock" directions but attach yarn on top of foot rather than bottom of foot. Substitute bottom for top, and top for bottom when reading directions to reverse direction of toe shaping.

RED HOT

By Janet Rehfeldt

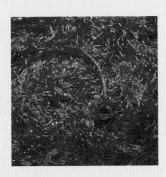

Crocheting with eyelash yarn is different than crocheting with smooth yarn. Work stitches so that they are slightly loose and use your fingers to locate the opening for your crochet hook at the top of each stitch. Since it can be difficult to locate rows between the fuzzy eyelashes, measure your cuff in inches rather than rows. If you have to undo your stitches, hold the piece in one hand, working left to right, and gently pull yarn forward, then back, in the same direction as if you were crocheting.

Featured Techniques

This pattern features the top-down method, the sideways single crochet cuff, and the heel flap with gusset.

Featured Stitches

Chain (ch)

Back loop (bl)

Half double crochet (hdc)

Single crochet (sc)

Single crochet decrease (sc2tog); page 11

Slip stitch (sl st)

Materials

1 (1, 1, 1) balls Adriafil Stars (50% viscose, 50% nylon; 50 g, 72 yds per ball), color 87 Red

2 (2, 2, 3) balls Plymouth Dreambaby D.K. (50% microfiber, 50% nylon; 50 g, 183 yds per ball), color 108 Red

Size E (3.5 mm) hook (or size required to obtain gauge) for leg, heel, and foot

Size H (5.0 mm) hook for cuff

3 stitch markers

Finished Dimensions
(WITH SOCK FOLDED FLAT)

Due to the stretch in the leg pattern, we recommend that you follow the pattern directions for the measurement that most closely matches your foot circumference.

Cir of leg (unstretched): 7¼ (8, 9, 9¾)"

Cir of foot (unstretched): 6¼ (7, 8, 9)"

Floor to cuff: 8"

Gauge

4.25 sts and 6 rnds = 1" in leg pat with Dreambaby and size E hook

7 sts and 5 rnds = 1" in foot pat with Dreambaby and size E hook

> Note: Unless otherwise instructed, do not sl st rnds closed, and do not ch 1 at beg of rnds and rows.

Cuff

Row 1: With size H hook and Stars yarn, ch 7, sc in bl of second ch from hook, sc in bl of each ch, turn. [6 sc]

Row 2: Ch 1, sc in bl of first sc, sc in bl of each sc across, turn. [6 sc]

Rep row 2 until piece measures 7 (8, 9, 10)" from beg.

Leg

Rnd 1: Change to size E hook and Dreambaby yarn, work 30 (34, 38, 42) sc evenly along one long edge of cuff, sl st in first sc to close rnd. Sew cuff closed (see page 12).

Rnd 2: (Sc, ch 1) in first sc, *(sc, ch 1) in next sc, rep from * around.

Rnds 3–5: *(Sc, ch 1) in next sc, sk ch sp*, rep from * to * around.

Rnd 6: Sk first sc, sc in next ch st, *(sc, ch 1) in next sc, sk ch sp*, rep from * to * around.

Rnds 7–11: Rep rnd 3.

Rep rnds 6–11 for pat st until piece measures 5" from beg incl cuff.

Heel

Row 1: Sc in next ch sp, PM, sc in next 2 sc, *sc in ch sp, sc in next 2 sc, rep from * to * 5 (6, 7, 7) times, turn. [21 (24, 27, 27) sc]

Row 2: Ch 1, sc in first sc and in each sc across.

Rep row 2 until heel measures 2¾" to 3" from beg, end with a WS row. Remove marker.

Heel Turn

Row 1 (RS): Ch 1, sc in first 2 sc, sc2tog twice, sc in next 2 (4, 5, 5) sc, sc2tog twice, sc in next 3 (4, 6, 6) sc, sc2tog twice, sc in last 2 sc, turn. [15, (18, 21, 21) sc]

Rows 2–3: Ch 1, sc in first 2 sc, sc2tog twice, sc to last 6 sts, sc2tog twice, sc in last 2 sc, turn. [7 (10, 13, 13) sc at end of row 3]

Row 4: Ch 1, sc in first 2 (4, 4, 4) sc, sc2tog 1 (1, 2, 2) times, sc in rem sc. Turn. [6 (9, 11, 11) sc]

Gusset

Rnd 1 (RS): Sc in each of 6 (9, 11, 11) heel sts, work 12 (12, 14, 14) sc evenly along right edge of heel flap, PM in last sc, sc2tog over first ch sp and sc on foot front (counts as 1 minicluster), *(sc, hdc) in next sc, sk ch sp*, rep from * to * 12 (14, 16, 19) times, sc2tog over last 2 sc on foot front skipping ch sp (counts as 1 minicluster), work 11 (12, 14, 14) sc evenly along left side edge of heel flap, PM in first sc on left side of heel, PM in last sc to mark beg of rnds. [29 (33, 39, 39) sc; 15 (17, 19, 21) minicluster sts]

Rnd 2: Sc to 1 st prior to first marker at gusset, sc2tog, (sc, hdc) in each sc on foot front, sk all hdc, sc2tog at next gusset marker, sc in rem heel sts. [27 (31, 37, 37) sc; 15 (17, 19, 21) minicluster sts]

Rep rnd 2 until 15 (17, 19, 21) sc rem with 15 (17, 19, 21) miniclusters. Remove gusset markers.

Foot

Rnd 1: Sc in each sc around right side of heel, work in pat across foot front, *(sc, hdc) in next sc on heel, sk 1 sc*, rep from * to * 5 (6, 7, 8) times to last 3 sc on heel, sc2tog over next 2 sc, hdc in same st, sk last sc. PM to mark beg of rnds. [22 (25, 28, 31) miniclusters]

Rnd 2: *(Sc, hdc) in next sc, sk next hdc*, rep from * to * around. [22 (25, 28, 31) miniclusters]

Rep rnd 2 for pat st until foot measures 2½" from longest toe.

Next rnd: Sc in each st around. [44 (50, 56, 62) sc]

Shape Toe

PM at each side edge. Move markers after each rnd to keep at side edges of sock.

Rnd 1: Sc to 1 st prior to first marker, sc2tog, sc in next sc, sc2tog, sc to 1 st prior to next marker, sc2tog, sc in next sc, sc2tog (partial rnd to set up toe). [40 (46, 52, 58) sc]

Rnd 2: Sc to 1 st prior to first marker, sc2tog, sc in next sc, sc2tog, sc to 1 st prior to next marker, sc2tog, sc in next sc, sc2tog. [36 (42, 48, 54) sc]

Rep rnd 2 until 20 (22, 24, 26) sts rem. Fasten off. Sew toe.

HARLEQUIN CABLES

By Janet Rehfeldt

Harlequin Cables uses cleverly placed front-post double crochet stitches in two colors to create light and airy cables. When you end the first round of the Fair Isle pattern on the foot, you will appear to end with two black blocks together. However, as you change to white for the next two stitches, they naturally spiral up and into the next round, resulting in a houndstooth check appearance. If you use the Lion Brand yarn listed for the pattern, you will get several pairs of socks from one skein of each color. The foot pattern compensates for the stretch in the yarn and stitch structure, creating a design that fits snugly.

Featured Techniques

This pattern features the top-down method, the sideways slip stitch cuff, and the heel flap with gusset.

Featured Stitches

Chain (ch)

Crossed cable pattern; page 11

Double crochet (dc)

Front-post double crochet (FPDC); page 10

Half double crochet (hdc)

Half double crochet decrease (hdc2tog); page 12

Single crochet (sc)

Single crochet decrease (sc2tog); page 11

Slip stitch (sl st)

Materials

1 ball Lion Brand Wool-Ease Sportweight (80% acrylic, 20% wool; 140 g, 435 yds) in each of 153 Black and 301 White Multi

Size E (3.5 mm) hook for heel and foot (or size required to obtain gauge)

Size G (4.0 mm) hook for cuff and leg

3 stitch markers

Finished Dimensions
(WITH SOCK FOLDED FLAT)

Cir of leg (unstretched): 7¼ (8, 8¾, 9½)"

Cir of foot (unstretched): 6¾ (7½, 8¼, 8¾)"

Floor to cuff: 9"

Gauge

1.75 crossed cables and 5 rnds = 1" with size G hook in leg pat

5.25 sts and 4.5 rnds = 1" with size E hook in foot pat

 Note: Unless otherwise instructed, do not sl st rnds closed, and do not ch 1 at beg of rnds and rows.

Cuff

Row 1: With black and size G hook, ch 6, sl st in second ch from hook, *sl st in bl of next ch, rep from * across, turn. [5 sl st]

Rows 2 and 3: Ch 1, sl st in bl of first sl st and each st across, turn.

Row 4: Ch 1, sl st in bl of first sl st and each st across, changing color on last st, turn.

Rep rows 1–4, working 4 rows black then 4 rows white for 68 (68, 76, 76) rows total, end with 4 rows of white. Change to black.

Leg

Work FPDC around prev dc, not prev FPDC (see crossed cable pattern on page 11).

Rnd 1: Pivot cuff to work along long edge of cuff. With black, work 39 (42, 45, 48) sc evenly spaced along cuff, join with sl st in first sc. Sew cuff closed (see page 12).

Rnd 2: Sc in each sc around.

Rnd 3: *Sk 2 sc, dc in next sc, ch 1, dc in first skipped sc*, rep from * to * around. [13 (14, 15, 16) dc crosses]

Rnd 4: With white, sc in each st and each ch-1 sp around. [39 (42, 45, 48) sc]

Rnd 5: *Sk 2 sc, dc in next sc, ch 1, working in front of dc just made, FPDC around dc 2 rows below first skipped st*, rep from * to * around.

Rnd 6: With black, sc in each st and each ch-1 sp around.

Rnd 7: *Sk 2 sc, dc in next sc, ch 1, working in front of dc just made, FPDC around dc 2 rows below first skipped st*, rep from * to * around.

Rep rnds 4–7 another 3 times, end with black.

Next rnd: Sc in each st and each ch-1 sp around. Fasten off white only.

Heel

Row 1 (RS): With size E hook and black, sc in each of next 20 (20, 22, 22) sts, turn.

Row 2: Ch 1, sc in first sc and each sc across, turn.

Rep row 2 until heel measures 2¾" to 3", end with a WS row.

Heel Turn

Row 1 (RS): Ch 1, sc in first sc, sc2tog twice, *sc in each of next 3 (3, 4, 4) sc, sc2tog twice*, rep from * to * once, sc in last sc, turn. [14 (14, 16, 16) sc]

Row 2: Ch 1, sc in first sc, sc2tog, *sc in each of next 3 (3, 4, 4) sc, sc2tog*, rep from * to * once, sc in last sc, turn. [11 (11, 13, 13) sc]

Row 3: Ch 1, sc in first sc, sc2tog, sc in each of next 1 (1, 2, 2) sc, sc2tog, sc in each of next 2 (2, 3, 3) sc, sc2tog, sc in last sc. Do not turn. [8 (8, 10, 10) sc]

Gusset

Rnd 1 (RS): Work 14 sc evenly along right edge of heel flap, PM, sc across 19 (22, 23, 26) front foot sts, work 14 sc evenly along left side edge of heel flap, PM in first sc on left side of heel, sc in 8 (8, 10, 10) heel sts changing to white on last sc, PM in last sc made to mark beg of rnds. [55 (58, 61, 64) sts]

Rnd 2: With white, hdc in each sc to 3 sts prior to first gusset marker, hdc2tog twice, hdc across foot front, hdc2tog twice at next gusset marker, hdc in rem heel sts. [51 (54, 57, 60) hdc]

Rnd 3: Sc in each hdc around.

Rnds 4 and 5: Rep rnds 2 and 3. [47 (50, 53, 56) sts at end of rnd 5]

Rnd 6: Rep rnd 2. [43 (46, 49, 52) hdc]

Rnd 7: Sc in each hdc to 3 sts prior to first gusset marker, sc2tog twice, sc across foot front sts, sc2tog twice at next gusset marker, sc in rem heel sts. [39 (42, 45, 48) sc]

Rnd 8: Hdc in each sc to 3 (3, 1, 1) sts prior to first gusset marker, hdc2tog 2 (2, 1, 1) times, hdc across foot front sts, hdc2tog 2 (2, 1, 1) times, at next gusset marker, hdc in rem heel sts. [35 (38, 43, 46) hdc]

Rnd 9: Sc around to center back of foot, sc2tog 1 (0, 1, 0) times. [34 (38, 42, 46) sc]

Remove gusset markers.

Foot

Do not fasten off white. Insert hook into the st to the right of the post. When changing from black to white, it will appear as if the first white st is worked between a black and white st of the prev rnd and vice versa when changing from white to black (see "Changing Colors" on page 9).

Rnd 1: Sc in next sc, change to black, work black hdc in each of next 2 sts, *white hdc in each of next 2 sts, black hdc in each of next 2 sts*, rep from * to * around foot, do not join. [34 (38, 42, 46) hdc]

Rnds 2–5 (6, 6, 7): Work 2 hdc in white, 2 hdc in black, working white over black and black over white for 5 (6, 6, 7) rnds. End with black. At end of rnd 5 (6, 6, 7), sl st into next hdc with white. Fasten off black, leave a 3" to 6" tail.

Next rnd: With white, sc in each st around.

Next rnd: Hdc in each sc around.

Rep last 2 rnds until sock measures 2" from longest toe, end with hdc rnd. Change to black.

Shape Toe

PM at each side edge. Move markers with each rnd to keep them at side edges of toe.

Rnd 1: Sc to 2 sts prior to first marker, sc2tog, sc in next st, sc2tog, sc to 2 sts prior to next marker, sc2tog, sc in next st, sc2tog (partial rnd to set up toe). [30 (34, 38, 42) sc]

Rnd 2: Sc to 2 sts prior to first marker, sc2tog, sc in next st, sc2tog, sc to 2 sts prior to next marker, sc2tog, sc in next st, sc2tog. [26 (30, 34, 38) sc]

Rep rnd 2 until 18 (18, 22, 22) sts rem.

Fasten off. Sew toe.

WIGGLY TOES

By Mary Jane Wood

Whether you crochet each toe in a different color or all in the same color, these fanciful socks will have your toes wiggling and your feet happily dancing. Each toe in this sock can be crocheted to fit the length and width of your toes.

Featured Techniques

This pattern features the top-down method, the side-to-side leg, and the heel flap with gusset.

Featured Stitches

Back loop (bl)

Chain (ch)

Front loop (fl)

Half double crochet (hdc)

Half double crochet decrease (hdc2tog); page 12

Reverse single crochet (rsc)

Single crochet (sc)

Single crochet decrease (sc2tog); page 11

Slip stitch (sl st)

Materials

Multicolor-Toes Version

2 (2, 2, 3) balls Stahl Sche Wolle Socka Color (75% wool, 25% nylon; 50 g, 205 m per ball), color 9133 Multicolor

25 yds each of Stahl Sche Wolle Socka Color in solid colors red, yellow, green, blue, and pink for toes

One-Yarn Version

2 (2, 2, 3) balls Schachenmayr Regia Mini Ringel Color (75% wool, 25% nylon; 50 g, 210 m per ball), color 5217

Both Versions

Size E (3.50 mm) hook (or hook required to obtain gauge)

Finished Dimensions
(WITH SOCK FOLDED FLAT)

Cir of leg (unstretched): 6¾ (7¾, 9, 10¼)"

Cir of foot (unstretched): 6¾ (7½, 8, 9)"

Floor to cuff: 9¾"

Gauge

5.666 sts = 1" in pat st for leg ribbing and foot

4 rows = 1" in leg pat

4.25 rnds = 1" in foot pat

Pattern Stitch for Foot, Gusset, and Toes

Rnd 1: *Sc in next st, hdc in next st*, rep from * to * around.

Rnd 2: *Sc in next sc, hdc in next hdc*, rep from * to * around.

Rep rnd 2.

> Note: Unless otherwise instructed, do not sl st rnds closed, and do not ch 1 at beg of rnds and rows.